ACROSS THE WATER

Cover Photograph: William and Ann B. Cluett Family Group, Troy, N.Y., c. 1867

Seated foreground, left to right: John William Alfred Cluett (J.W. A. or Alfred), Mrs. J.W.A. (Lillie Bontecou) Cluett, George B. Cluett.

Seated middle , left to right: Mrs. Mulford (Joseph Mulford's mother), Edmund Cluett, Mrs. George B. (Amanda Rockwell) Cluett, Mary Bywater Lewis (Ann B. Cluett's sister).

Standing background, left to right: Rev. Joseph N. Mulford, Mary Cluett Mulford, William Cluett, Ann Bywater Cluett.

Seated background, looking to right: Robert Cluett.

Missing Cluett Siblings: Emily Cluett Cadby and husband John Harford Cadby (in England), and Frederick Cluett and wife Fannie (Francis Amelia Bishop).

Yet to join the family are Robert and Edmund's wives, Elizabeth Marchisi and Mary Alice Stone.

[A print of this photograph is in the archives of the Hart Cluett Museum, Troy, N.Y.]

ACROSS THE WATER

Debt, Faith and Fortune
In the Cluett Cadby Letters
1850-1869

MARJORIE CLUETT SEGUIN

2022

ISBN: 978-0-9940106-9-8

Title: Across the Water: Debt, Faith and Fortune
In the Cluett Cadby Letters, 1850-1869

Author: Marjorie Cluett Seguin

Publisher: Marjorie Cluett Seguin
Prince Edward County, Ontario, Canada. 2022

Comments, inquiries and requests for copies of this book can be sent by email to the author:
marjorie@ontariohistory.ca

This book is available at local bookstores, from major online book retailers, and at www.ontariohistory.ca

Front cover image: William and Ann B. Cluett Family Group. Troy, N.Y. c.1867 [Courtesy of the Hart Cluett Museum]
Back cover image: "Northern View of Troy, N.Y., from Mount Olympus", [From *Historical Collections of the State of New York*, by John W. Barber and Henry Howe. New York, 1851.]

Table of Contents

ACKNOWLEDGEMENTS

A few years ago I received a binder of family letters dating back to 1850. The letters had come to me courtesy of Virginia (Ginny) Horger Grogan, via my father. Thus began an intense interest for me in the lives of my Cluett ancestors.

It is thanks to the work of Ginny Grogan that this publication is possible. Ginny is a descendant of Emily Cluett Cadby (b. 1830), the Cluett daughter who stayed behind in England when the rest of her family migrated to America in 1850, and to whom and from whom most of these letters were written. Due to Ginny's diligence in gathering the letters, transcribing them, and sharing them with her extended family, we are able to read the Cluett Cadby letters here.

Starting in the 1980's, with help from her cousin, Emily Rodemann, Ginny reproduced and shared with her wider family what letters, family records and research had been collected. Individuals in other branches of the family (grandsons of George B. Cluett, Gorham and John Parmenter Cluett) had also copied and shared some of the letters and other documents in the 1960's, which Ginny added to her own group. Ginny subsequently donated the letters she had to the Hart Cluett Museum in Troy, New York.

My father, Robert Cluett IV, has spent years reflecting on and writing about his family heritage (see *The Gold Of Troy*, 2003), and he sought a copy of the letters. After obtaining a set of the transcribed letters from his third cousin Ginny, he reproduced them for his family.

Finding the letters of interest, and with Ginny's support in sharing her transcriptions and digital copies of the original letters, I finished digitizing the group of letters in 2017, and began to write down my own observations, with the idea of making the letters more broadly available in print.

This book is the result of five generations of Cluetts seeing value in the words of their forebears. I owe thanks to those who read and saved the letters, and passed them on for others to see.

Many thanks to my husband, Marc Seguin, for his tireless work on the layout of this book, and for his feedback and editing input. His dedication has helped to make this book a more serious and elegant enterprise than it otherwise would have been.

Finally, thanks are due to the Hart Cluett Museum and the Rensselaer County Historical Society of Troy, New York, for archiving the Cluett Cadby letters, and for supporting individuals, such as me, interested in researching the diverse history of the people of Troy. Without these guardians of history, lay and professional, such undertakings would not be possible.

My apologies for any errors in family history or other matters of fact. The opinions contained herein are wholly my own! I welcome correspondence on any of the content here, or anything related to Cluett family history. With many thanks,

Marjorie Cluett Seguin 2022
Consecon, Ontario, Canada
marjorie@ontariohistory.ca

Across the Water

ACROSS THE WATER: DEBT, FAITH AND FORTUNE

Introduction

Stored in the archives of the Hart Cluett Museum in Troy, New York, a group of forty-three letters traces the correspondence amongst members of a family separated by a trans-Atlantic move in the middle of the 19th Century.

The story begins with a tearing apart, as eight of nine members of the Cluett family leave their home in England, fleeing to America in secret while one daughter stays behind.

Strangled by debt and with a wife and seven children to care for, William Cluett feared for the future of his family in England in 1850. A well-read and upstanding citizen, church-elder and community member, he made the shocking decision to duck out on his debts from his business as a bookseller in Birmingham, and to secretly depart on a ship bound for America with his wife and six of his children. Eldest daughter Emily stayed in England, as she was engaged to be married to John Cadby, an associate of her father's in the book-selling business.

From the moment of departure from England, father William and daughter Emily write letters to each other on the subject of his flight from his debts, which effectively leaves his daughter and future son-in-law to face the creditors and do what they could to pay the debts down.

About William's decision, in the first letter to her father after he has left for America, Emily writes, "*All say 'you are the last Man in the world of whom they should have expected to hear such things.'*"

While working to gain a foothold in their new home of Troy, New York, the Cluetts are conscious of their shame and they fear exposure of their decision to flee England while owing money. William's wish to resume work as a lay preacher particularly arouses family fear of exposure. However, he takes on preaching jobs, finds paid work and they carry on.

After struggling for a few years in Troy, the Cluetts begin to prosper. In fact, they begin to prosper enormously as the sons become adult and work in business along with their father or enter other businesses themselves.

Within a generation, the family is phenomenally successful, pillars of the community, both financially, and in their good works. They are active in various churches, and donate heavily to community projects, buildings and worthy endeavors.

The Cluett family became central in the city of Troy at a time of great growth and prosperity in the north-eastern United States. Each of the Cluett offspring in America made great contributions to the church and to the civic life of the town — donating funds, helping to found community institutions, volunteering in musical and administrative positions both in the religious and the political life of the city. The moral aspiration of the individuals rings out in the letters, but each of them knows of the shame and ignominy with which they fled England.

The family letters are full of counsel to be faithful and fervent in Christian practice, and to remember God in everything. But underneath, the lives of the Cluetts in Troy are built on a lie about their reason for coming to America.

William, his wife Ann and their children work together to keep their past a secret. Ann asks their daughter Emily in England to lie about their whereabouts, to give no one a forwarding address and to work to mislead others as to their actual residence.

As the years pass, the family 'makes good' on two fronts in America. Their financial, religious, and civic success is well known in the family and in the city of Troy. But more importantly the family appears to 'make good' on the moral front. By Letter #23, in 1859, William says "[we] *are known as a Model family*", and, amazingly, ("*I scarcely know how,*") they are "*able to get credit for almost any amount.*"

And while William appears to have some torments in conscience about his actions, this does not necessarily translate into freeing up some of the wealth he is soon able to accumulate; writing letters to Emily listing their furnishings, the state of their house, and the sizes of their new stores.

As William moves further away in time from his original shame, and as he and his offspring become more well established, both materially and socially, family concern about his earlier transgressions and the obligations they carry seems to lessen. Seventeen years after migrating the debts had still not been paid off.

William and Ann Cluett did not (and nor did their communities) see material wealth as being inconsistent with spiritual wealth. And while it is clear that the children all dedicated themselves to good works, at the same time material wealth remained a huge goal in the family.

While descendants of William and Ann have concluded that the debts that the family left behind would certainly have been repaid, it is not clear that this is the case. The letters and accompanying documents provide some interesting disjunctions as to when and how and whether the debts were paid.

In looking at the family now, so many generations later, it appears that the burden of shame was part of what motivated William's children to achieve so extraordinarily. They had to get past not just their poverty but the sense that they had fallen from grace. The only way to do that in America was to 'establish a character' — for William to keep quiet about the debts he left behind, and to carry the secret through to death.

William's obituary is testament to his lifelong goal of re-establishing his place in the eyes of the world as an upstanding and righteous man. He is described as a man known for the "*purity of his heart and the integrity of his intentions*", and his "*pure, straight forward, even-handed life*". In sum, after William's death at 83, "*in all those long years there be naught but good recorded.*"

William's understandably glowing obituary is in part the product of the aphorism, *De mortuis nihil nisi bonum* (Of the dead, say nothing but good), but to the extent that it describes William as above sin, it is an illustration of what he sought to do in his life — which was to hide his original misdemeanor and to rise above the shattered moral reputation he left in England.

Even now, it seems that family members and admirers in the community seek to preserve the memory of the Cluett family as 'blameless'. Their achievements are staggering, and yet the linking of those achievements with moral perfection is a fallacy.

What is the connection between spiritual aspiration, shame, and money? What is the connection between ambition, and a fervent Christianity?

The Cluett family was able to reunite only once, in Troy, New York, fifteen years after emigrating, when daughter Emily traveled to Troy in late 1865. However, within five years of her visit to America, Emily was dead, along with her eleventh child, leaving husband John Cadby and ten children behind in 1870. A year later, John moved to America with his children.

And so, twenty years after the family's migration, the correspondence across the ocean ended, the need for writing now gone. Grieving the loss of Emily, family members on both sides of the Atlantic kept the letters.

The letters tell the story of one family, simultaneously drawn to money and by their faith. And while these letters are particular to that family, they speak in a voice that resonates beyond the individuals who corresponded after a sudden parting, thereafter always divided by the sea.

Accompanying the letters are related documents, historical background, contributions from other descendants and a commentary on William's debt.

The Letters

Overview of the Letters

When I first read the set of correspondence amongst members of my ancestral Cluett family, I felt that I was entering their world. Each writes with a candour and an expressiveness, a comfort with words and their uses, that is compelling.

At the centre of the correspondence lie two primary tensions: the pain of separation between migrating family and the daughter left behind in England, and the goal of escaping debt in order to make a better life for the six out of seven children who left for America. These tensions are central in the letters — their intense wish to be reunited, coupled with the powerful desire to rise above financial disaster and, perhaps more importantly, to get beyond the moral downfall of fleeing creditors to begin anew.

Given that the family was deeply religious, and already sincerely engaged with the growth and propagation of the Christian faith in England, the uncomfortable fact that they fled England in order to avoid repayment of debts sits both stated and silent throughout the course of their correspondence.

Astonishingly, the family goes from comfortable middle class (albeit overwhelmed with debt in England), to not just moral pillars of their new community of Troy, New York, but business pillars as well. Father and two sons do well in the music business, and three other sons join and then exponentially expand the cuff and collar business they work in, and become truly wealthy.

But in all of this spiritual and fiscal aspiration is the still-unfinished business of the debts, which remain unpaid through at least their first seventeen years of financial and family growth in America. Whether the debts were ever fully paid off remains an unknown.

The letters interest me both because they are a compelling window into the lives of people who clearly loved and supported each other and who were committed to making the most of their resources and gifts, but also because of the moral tension that is set up in their spiritual aspirations coupled with their secret unpaid debt. That goal of moral and social greatness was both grasped and shared by their immediate descendants, and was a goal which still resonated in my branch of the Cluett family more than one hundred years later.

I am interested in that place of human foible — the secret that they strove to keep buried, and the energy they put into building their new lives, materially and religiously, while being loathe to face their financial obligations on the other side of the water.

Here enclosed are the letters, written over a span of nineteen years, covering the period during which the Cluetts got established in America; rose in business and in community involvement, and the children grew to adulthood, married, and began to have families of their own.

List of Letters

The characters in (parentheses) correspond to the those that were penciled onto the original letters by Virginia Grogan. These letters are now in the Hart Cluett Museum archives. Archived letters with no number are marked here as (x). [List created by Virginia Grogan.]

Letter	Date	From	To	Notes
#1 (1)	June 26, 1850	FROM Emily	TO mother Ann	Family has just left England
#2 (2)	June 26, 1850	FROM Emily	TO father William	
#3 (3)	June 26 [1850]	FROM Ann	TO daughter Emily	On ship
#4 (4)	[Spring 1851]	FROM Ann	TO Emily	News of boys
#5 (4)	[Spring 1851]	FROM George	TO sister Emily	
#6 (4)	[Spring 1851]	FROM Mary	TO sister Emily	
#7 (5)	May 6, 1851	FROM Ann	TO Emily	William, traveling preacher
#8 (5)	May 6, 1851	FROM Mary	TO Emily	
#9 (6)	Aug. 20, 1851	FROM Ann	TO Emily	Mary's situation; food
#10 (x)	Sept. 4, 1851	FROM William	TO daughter Emily	
#11 (x)	Sept. 4, 1851	FROM William	TO son-in-law John	
#12 (7)	Oct., 1852	FROM Mary	TO Emily	Church
#13 (8)	Nov., 1852	FROM Mary	TO Emily	Family performing
#14 (8)	Nov., 1852	FROM Ann	TO Emily	Mary's new clothes
#15 (9)	Mar. 1, 1854	FROM Alfred	TO sister Emily	
#16 (x)	Mar. 4, 1855	FROM Ann	TO Emily	
#17 (10)	Apr. 14, 1855	FROM Mary	TO Emily	Music and religion
#18 (10)	Apr. 14, 1855	FROM Mary	TO brother-in-law John	Moving to a new house
#19 (11)	Apr. 29, 1856	FROM Mary	TO Emily	Moving to a new house
#20 (12)	Aug. 28, 1856	FROM Mary	TO Emily	

Letter	Date	From	To	Notes
#21 (13)	1857	FROM Frederick	TO sister Emily	Excursion to Hudson
#22 (13)	1857	FROM Ann	TO Emily	
#23 (14)	Oct. 30 [1858/9]	FROM William	TO Emily	Family is esteemed; William meets cousins in Philadelphia
#24 (x)	July 8, 1862	FROM William	TO Emily	After the Great Fire
#25 (15)	Aug. 13, 1862	FROM Ann	TO Emily	Polly visiting; Alfred and George have girl friends
#26 (16)	Sept. 19, 1863	FROM William	TO son-in-law John	
#27 (A)	1864?	FROM Mary	TO Emily	married life
#28 (B)	1864?	FROM Ann	TO Emily	"over eighth difficulty"
#29 (C)	1864?	FROM Ann	TO Emily	
#30 (16a)	Oct., 1864	FROM Ann	TO John	Ann tries to persuade John to bring his family to America [middle 4 pages of a letter found in Hart Cluett Museum, 2021]
#31 (17)	Nov. 14, 1864	FROM George	TO Emily	George's wife has died
#32 (18)	May 8, 1865	FROM Mary	TO Emily	Mary's foster daughter
#33 (19)	Jan. 3, 1866	FROM Mary	TO Emily	After a visit by Emily
#34 (20)	Apr., 1867	FROM Ann	TO Emily	Alfred's baby died; Fred has a baby
#35 (21)	Apr. 15, 1867	FROM William	TO Emily	William's businesses
#36 (22)	Nov. 2, 1868	FROM Mary	TO Emily	Emily's 10th child Lillian is born
#37 (23)	July 15, 1869	FROM Emily	TO brother George	George offers to bring home two of Emily's children
#38 (24)	Aug. 9, 1869	FROM Mary	TO Emily	Freddie's wife
#39 (25)	Sept. 3, 1869	FROM Emily	TO George	Her children left for Troy
#40 (26)	Sept. 3, 1869	FROM George	TO John and Emily	
#41 (27)	Sept. 5, 1869	FROM Emily	TO George and Amanda	Relieved children have arrived
#42 (28)	Sept. 13, 1869	FROM Emily	TO daughters Pollie and Emmie	
#43 (29)	Nov. 7, 1869	FROM Amanda	TO sister-in-law Emily	This is the last known letter

A Note About the Letters

The letters are arranged chronologically, and are written between Emily Cluett (later Cadby) in England, and her parents and siblings in America, between 1850 and 1869. Spelling and punctuation are retained as written in the letters.

Multiple dashes -------------- indicate obscured or faded text that could not be transcribed. Square brackets [...] denote annotations inserted by the transcriber.

Names and ages of family members at the time of their migration, in June of 1850, when they departed from Liverpool, England, on the sailing ship *Catherine*, bound for New York City:

PARENTS:

William Cluett, b. 1806	43 years old
Ann Bywater Cluett, b. 1805	44 years old

CHILDREN:

Emily Cluett (later Cadby) b. 1830 *Emily remained in England and married John Harford Cadby.*	20 years old
James William Alfred (Alfred) Cluett b. 1834 *Alfred later married Lillie Bontecou.*	16 years old
Mary Harris Cluett (later Mulford) b. 1836 *Mary later married her second cousin, Rev. Joseph Mulford.*	14 years old
George Bywater Cluett b. 1838 *George later married Sarah Bontecou Golden, then Amanda Rockwell Fisher.*	12 years old
Edmund Cluett b. 1840 *Edmund later married Mary Mattice, then Alice Stone.*	10 years old
Frederick Cluett b. 1842 *Fred later married Francis (Fannie) Bishop.*	8 years old
Robert b. 1844 *Robert later married Elizabeth (Lizzie) Marchisi.*	6 years old

Letter #1 – Daughter Emily to mother Ann

In the opening letters, Emily Cluett copes with the grief, shock and fall-out from her family's sudden departure, which she expresses to her parents, now en route to America. It is clear that Emily knew the rest of the family were leaving when they said goodbye as the family sailed for America.

Emily asks her mother to tell her the whole story about William's debts and the reason for the family flight from England, and she describes the beginning of the social cost for the family member who has stayed behind at Wolverhampton. *"My mind has suffered from the treatment of a few in W. Hampton….",* says Emily.

June 26, 1850

My very dear Mother,

My hand trembles so much, I can scarcely write and I am discouraged by the thought that in all probability your eyes will never glance over these pages, even should they be fortunate enough to reach my dear father. I have had so many fears lest the voyage should prove too much for your weak body, that I believe my mind is prepared for the worst. Oh! how many times in a day and night do I think and dream of you, wondering what you are all doing, and wherever you all are; how would it lessen my trials could I but be assured you were all safe. No one can conceive how my heart aches when I think of our once happy home, our bright fireside, surrounded as it was by all those I loved; what would I not give to see once more the smiles of all those beloved faces, which seem to me now far dearer than my own life. I dare not encourage hope, or that would sometimes cheer me. Your Portrait I have seen but few times since your departure I know not why I cannot bear to see it, when I have summoned courage enough just to take one look, I have had to pay dearly for it, and after all have closed it up in bitter disappointment. It has no life! Often do I start up during the day and night and think I hear you call me as you were wont to do, but I will say no more on this, or else these pages would contain an enumeration of my griefs on your account. I have no doubt I should be a great deal more happy and satisfied if I could hear of your safe arrival in New York. Whenever my father or any of the others write, let them not fail to tell me the whole truth, however dreadful the truth may be. As far as my own circumstances are concerned, I am very comfortable. It has taken me three weeks to settle affairs at W. Hampton [Wolverhampton], and I have been in such a continual whirl of bustle and business I have had very little time for thinking. I am now in Birmingham learning a business. I have only an hour in the morning and another in the evening to call my own, except Sundays which I have entirely for myself. I had holiday yesterday afternoon, or I should not have written this. You need not be anxious on ------------------------ have everything I need, and everybody is very kind ---------------------------------- well in health, and I believe if you knew you were ----------------------------------- I should be better in spirits than I have been for ------------------------- --------------- I had not the remotest idea of writing until ------------ ------------------------------ before I began, and this is to be posted tomorrow --------------------------------------- be delayed a week, therefore I had not time --- and Aunt Lewis know anything about it, my Ann --------------------------- ------- poorly, she has not got better so rapidly as you ----------------- ------------------------ in a great measure I believe to be ---------------------------------- is not well, he too thinks a great ------- -------------------- and is often exceedingly low about you all. John -

------------------------------ best love to all, the shop is as usual, business ------------------------------------ flat as I expected it to be this time of the year. John ------------------------------------ poorly; the week before last I was spending a few days at Copes, and one evening he went accompanied by Tom Cope, John Kidyard and Mr. Carrington to bathe; they had not been gone long before John Kidyard came in quite exhausted with the news that Carrington was drowned. I daresay you will recollect him, he was just entering upon his 21st year a great comfort to his Mother, and beloved by all, a day or two before it took place he was talking about you saying he hoped you would have a prosperous voyage, that he thought drowning was an easy death and that if he were to die any other than a natural death he should prefer drowning. Poor fellow he was in the water more than half an hour, and the circumstances of the case were altogether as distressing as they could be, all who went with him had a narrow escape. It has given nerves a shock that time alone will recover.

Give my love to my dear Alfred, tell him I often fancy I see his form flitting about as I wend my way along the streets. I cannot tell him the grief I felt upon entering the office the day after you went, to find his fiddle in the corner. It must have been a bitter disappointment to him. I have put it up for him until I come to America. Give my love to my dear Mary. I am sure Taylors would have sent flowers if they had known of this, they are all expecting to hear from her. It seems Johnny was very much grieved to part with her, for I hear secretly, on that eventfull night he paced the yard for hours, in tears! My love to George and Edmund, and Frederick, I do hope that they will be good boys, and that their lives will be preserved, that I may see them once again. And lastly my love to my dearest little Bobby, I hope he is well, and God bless him, to tell him I love him very much, and pray for him every day. Tell them all to pray for me! two or three times every day. I commend you all into the hands of him who seeth and knoweth all things. I hope to hear from you soon, every particular, what you have met with, what were your provisions, who was the Captain, and crew, what health you have had and everything you can think of. I do not know what more I can tell you.

My mind has suffered much from the treatment of a few in W. Hampton. I believe I have some real friends in Birmingham. I am during the day occupied with two or three more girls of my own age, during the day I see many strange faces, and I have a bed room to myself a mile out of town. I fear mine is an indifferent composition. I have had to leave it many times, my feelings have so overpowered me. I expect a letter every day to tell me of the death of my Grandfather, his agonies cannot be greater, I saw him last week, he did not know me, and the doctor then said he would not survive the night. Give my love to my beloved Father. With what anguish do I think of the parting kiss. I fear while [I] write that you will never get this, and yet I have some hope that my father will go the New York post-office, and therfore I chance it. And now my dear my beloved Mother I send my love to you, would to God I were with you, when you send, let me have a lock of your hair.

I cannot say more, ------------------- the Lord support us all is the prayer of your disconsolate daughter.

Emily Cluett

Letter #2 – Daughter Emily to father William

Emily writes a separate letter to her father on the same day concerning the reasons for, and the effects of, his secret departure. Evidently she has been instructed by William to collect what money she can that is owed to him: "*Send an authority... all the debtors refuse to pay me.*" And with regard to paying off William's debts (which she is apparently also under instruction to do), "*a few of the smallest creditors I have paid... but there remains many yet to be paid.*"

As for William's reputation, Emily writes, "*The sudden and quiet way in which you disappeared has created great surprise in all who have heard of the affair and all say 'You are the last Man in the World of whom they should have expected to hear such things*".

Emily has received letters from lawyers and fielded the displeasure of William's peers. In these early letters it is clear that Emily has been left exposed both financially and socially by the behaviour of her father, and, under his instructions, has been left to take on the challenges.

Now at Birmingham June 26, 1850

My very dear Father

I send this by Mr. Cope's advice, though in an uncertainty as to whether it ever reaches you, to request you to send an authority, either to Mr. Pass, or me or someone else to receive the debts, which I cannot obtain by any means. All the Debtors with few exceptions refuse to pay me, as it is now generally known where you are. Furnsmore, Kittlesson, Harley, and some others will not pay any portion of it without a receipt from you. Mr. Smith has obtained a few of the smallest amounts but refuses to have anything more to do with the concern. Edwin has given up the keys to the Auction Rooms to Meredith who has got possession, so that all is loss there entirely. Mr Willim also has taken possession of the Bilston Auction Room with all that was in them, fixtures, crates of China and all he could find upon the premises.

A few of the smallest creditors I have paid as far as the money would hold out, but there remains many yet to be paid. Some of the money due to you, I can find no account of whatever and have no idea of the amount. All the property except Osborn's pictures, remains still in the Auction Rooms in ----- All that was yours I had removed to the House the day you went, and that, together with the whole of the Furniture only realised fifteen pounds!! And a very great deal of trouble I have gone through to get even that sum. I think I may say that untill this week I have never had one hour to call my own, scarcely for sleep, since you went. The sudden and quiet way in which you disappeared has created great surprise in all who have heard of the affair and all say "You are the last Man in the World of whom they should have expected to hear such things". Mr. Yateman heard of it the day after, and on the Sunday followed you to Liverpool in the hope of seeing you, solely for the purpose (I believe) of sympathizing with you, but could hear no tidings either of you or the vessel in which you were to sail. Both Mr. and Mrs. Yateman have been exceedingly kind to me, offering me a home at their house as long as I please, though I have never yet accepted it, neither do I intend, as I have a situation and am independent of every one.

I have had Lawyers letters from different parties in London, this morning I received a note from Washbourne requesting your address. Iliffe is enraged, though he has only troubled us once. I have given Lee and Dixon the bills you left for them, but neither of the bills had your signature affixed. Mr. Cope is very much displeased with you, he says he will never forgive you unless you write to him directly you land, he sends his love to all and when he knows where you are will be after you. It seems a long time since you went; and only three weeks! What an age. You will see me some of these days!

I am my dear father your affectionate daughter

Emily

Letter #3 – Mother Ann to daughter Emily, from the ship

Mother Ann, en route to America, writes to Emily from the ship. She is already looking forward to a better life: "*I am glad we came in the best cabins for we never should have endured it in the intermediate....*" Despite the family owing large sums of money, Ann aspires to have good surroundings and sees herself as peers with those in the better accommodation. Money and moral station are linked in her mind (and not in her mind alone.) She has set the past and William's actions behind her and is moving ahead without apparent guilt.

Near the banks of Newfoundland June 26 [1850]

My Dear Child

Mary has described a little of the smooth now for some of the rough. About one o'clock on the morning of Wednesday the first week of our voyage, the sea began to heave, and the ship to toss about at a stronger rate, when nearly every passenger on board was taken sick. Such a scene of confusion I never expected to witness. Clothes flying in all directions, cups and bottles, chairs and trays jumping about as though they were alive, and every one of our family sick but myself. Your father especially, he was very ill indeed. The steward came about daylight and took him out of the confusion, and laid him upon the Captains bed, where he remained till 9 oclock at night, none of us being able to go near him, for I was advised to keep in bed to prevent sickness, however I had a touch of it for about half an hour, but it was but slight. I am very very thankful to say, for I had every one to attend to, but very short of waiters, the stewardess who had only been two voyages before was as ill as any of them. I know not what I should have done but for a youth of about 14 years of age, nephew to a Catholic Priest who was also on Board, and at whose request he attended upon us. I never shall forget his kindness, for it was at a time of need.

Well after the bustle of the day we spent a tolerable comfortable night, and were all better next morning, though still very unwell. George and your father worst of all, indeed they were some days before they could either eat, or sit up. Bobby, Edmund, and Freddy were nearly well next day. Alfred & Mary were a little longer but got through very well.

Since then I have been very unwell, the sea air took a great affect upon me, some days I was not able to rise, or scarcely to eat anything. Now I am thankful to say my appetite is better, and I am well enough to be out on the deck most of the day. We live very well having plenty of corned beef at every meal and fowls and duck, or fresh mutton for dinner most days, and beautiful ham cooked before the fire for breakfast every morning, we are only stinted in one thing, and that is bread, we can have it only once a day, as there are more cabin passengers than usual, and there is so much to cook the oven cannot be spared for baking more than once a day. I manage myself to have some for every meal as I cannot bite the biscuits.

Our captain is I believe a very humane, though a passionate man, he is kind and polite to all, particularly obliging to me, allowing me privilege the others have no claim to, on account of age. He tells me I have only to give my orders to the steward, not only as to my own diet but to the dinner table in general, and they shall be obeyed. He is too a very vigilant man, exceedingly anxious for the welfare of both passengers and ship. While we were in the Channel he was up for whole nights together, it being a dangerous part of the voyage. I will just mention one or two instances of his kindness. It appears when a vessel leaves Liverpool, the poor Irish are apt to secrete themselves in nooks and corners of the ship in order to obtain a passage to New York. A steamer was hired to convey us about twenty miles away from the docks, and before the steamer left us 20 Irish men and women were found about the ship and sent back by the steamer. Three or four days after that two more men and two women were found nearly starved to death. The Captain was very much enraged and said he would leave them at a small uninhabited Island not far distant, and for that purpose ordered the long boats to be put in readiness to convey them thither, while the poor creatures were crying, and lamenting their sad fate. I felt very sorry for them, however we passed the Island and no notice was taken, but on the contrary they were ordered to be fed. I saw one a day or two after, and asked him if he would have the beef from which I made my tea, but he said he did not need it because the Captain ordered them plenty to eat.

Another instance is, an old Irish woman in the steerage who is more than 60 years of age and very poor was so prostrated by seasickness, that she was for some time not expected to rally, the Captain requested that nothing should be left undone that would be of service to her, so after great care she recovered. I saw her yesterday and asked how she was. She said she was getting round nicely, and that the Captain had sent her an excellent dinner from the cabin ever since her illness. The other day I heard him tell a servant to go and find a tall woman who was not well and tell her to send to the cabin for any nice thing she could fancy. He is very fond of Bobby, has him to sit by him at the head of the table, and given him all the nice bits. He also plays with him after at pitch and toss. Bobby has won 9 pence of his since we started.

The children are all happy enough in fine weather, in fact enjoy themselves very much, for it is delightful to be on deck on a fine day, but when it is wet it is rather dreary, especially for the children, as they have not room to play about. We have had beautiful weather part of the voyage, the other part has been sometimes stormy, at other times foggy and damp, which is exceedingly disagreeable. I am very glad we came in the best cabin for we never should have endured it in the intermediate. There are many respectable, and monied people here, one man has with him a thousand pounds, and others have tolerable sums, but oh how tiresome they find the voyage! I often walk down among them and hear their complaints, they say they never thought to have so much to pass through or they never would have come. There are some from Shropshire and other parts of England, but the greater part are from Ireland.

I forbear using soft expressions, it would do me no good to write or you to read them, but I must say I often wish I could know where you are, and what you are doing, though I am not over anxious about you, knowing that wherever you are, the Lord is with you. The children would be very miserable if they did not think you would follow us shortly, for they miss you very much. Give my kind love to John, Miss Taylor and all inquiring friends. I could say much more but my paper is full. I remain my Dear Emily your affect.

A. Cluett

Letter #4 – Ann to Emily

It is a year later when Ann writes Emily in the spring of 1851. Ann says, "*I hope you are not unhappy about things in general. Never mind the frowns and slights,*" presumably of the individuals affected by the unpaid debts, and by the censure of those who knew of William's actions.

About Bidyard and Taylor (business associates of William's) Ann says "*I am not surprised at Bidyard's behaviour to you but I am a little surprised at Taylor's…I feel very grateful to Mr. and Mrs. Cope for their kindness.*"

Regarding business for William in Troy, "*we have had a very flat winter and your father is almost tired of grocery.*" Ann adds, "*I have joined society now, and went to Chapel last Sunday for the first time. I am thankful we came to America, both as regards my health, and other circumstances.*"

Ann prefers not to refer to the actions of their family by name, instead calling the debts "*other circumstances.*" Her conscience seems to remain untroubled by the unpaid debts, and her faith appears to support this. Ann's lack of concern for the effects of their actions on others would seem to conflict with her Christian faith, and yet she herself does not express any sense of conflict about their actions.

[Spring 1851]

My dear Child,

I think it a very long time since I saw you, and how long it will yet be God alone knows. I should have written to you oftener, but I looked at the expence, and knowing that you heard from us through other channels, I thought it would not signify. However, I will endeavor to do better for the time to come. We are all, through the mercy of God, in tolerably good health. We have passed through the hottest and the coldest of our new climate. The winter has been very short, but part of it rather severe. It set in early Dec. when there fell a heavy snow. It was nearly a yard deep. At the same time it froze very hard, and continued frosty and clear till the beginning of Jan'y. It then began to thaw, and thawed in earnest for a week without rain. Then from that time until the beginning of Feb'y, we had fine dry pleasant weather. We then had a second winter. There was not so much snow, but it froze more intensely. I can assure you it was cold, and no mistake, for about a week. Since then it has been moderate, and some of the time very pleasant. And now the spring has set in, and the weather is beautiful.

I have passed through the winter very well considering all things, though I have one small attack of my complaint. I went one day into my chamber to make my bed. There was no fire in the room, and the water in the jug was frozen to a solid mass. I stayed to make my bed, but the cold seem to freeze me up. I was taken ill in the afternoon and was obliged to go to bed. I was better in the morning, but was unable to rise. However, through the mercy of my Heavenly Father, and without the help of a doctor, I was restored in a few days to my usual health.

I am sorry, my dear child, to hear that your eyesight is bad. I fear you will suffer great inconveniences from it as long as you live. I would advise you to purchase a pair of prescribes [?] and never sew or read without using them. You do not say what was the matter with you when you were unwell. I suppose it must have been your nirvs. I hope you are not unhappy about things in general. Never mind the frowns and slights…

(you must turn over two halves [2 pages of this letter] for I have made a mistake)

…of those who can't ----- smile upon you when fortune smiled. Their friendship is not worth having. I am not surprised at Bidyard's behavior towards you, though I am a little at Taylor's. I wish you had been more explicit about the latter. I feel very grateful to Mr. and Mrs. Cope for there kindness to you. Give my best love to them, and tell Mr. Cope he must not disappoint us. We shall all be most happy to see him and his brother and will use our utmost efforts to make them comfortable.

Respecting business, I have nothing very cheery to report. We have had a very flat winter, and your father is almost tired of grocery. I think he will give it up and deal in furniture alone, which pays much better. It is now all over with the cheap mutton and beef. We can't buy under ----- per pound, but we have a pretty good stock of salt ----- mutton, beef, and pork. The meat will not be cheap again until Autumn.

The children have all saved their toys except Edmund and he says I must tell you that the marbles were such moveable things that he lost them all on board the ship. He has not been well all the winter, nor able to stand the cold at all, while Freddy has gone out the coldest days we have had. They have both grown very much. Bobby has grown a great deal since you saw him and has become a savey little fellow. He often talks about you, and says you must come to America very soon.

How is John? I should like to see him. Give my kind love to him, and tell him he must prepare to come to America. He cannot do better than learn book keeping by double entry, he will be sure of a situation with a good salary. I know he likes bookselling better, but I am not sure he would succeed in that, and he must come here sooner or later. Present my love and thanks to Mrs. Tinkers. I wish it was in my power to reward her for her kindness to you. Whoever behaves kindly to my precious child is highly esteemed by me. I am sorry your Uncle Lewis is not coming earlier this summer. If he had come in the spring he would have been sure of a situation immediately. If he comes in the summer, he may have to wait a few weeks, or perhaps longer than that, before there is an opening. But there is no doubt of his ultimate success. I wish your father understood your uncle's business, it would be better than storekeeping.

I have joined society here, and went to Chapel last Sunday for the first time. I stood it very well, and hope now to be able to go regularly. I am thankful we came to America, both as regards my health, and other circumstances. From what you said in your letter we have been expecting one from your Uncle Lewis, but have not yet received one. Write soon and let me know exactly how you are.

I remain, my Dear Child,
Your affectionate Mother

Ann Cluett

~ ~ ~

Letter #5 – Brother George to sister Emily

This letter from George, age thirteen, was in the same envelope as Ann's letter. Brother George writes telling Emily,"*My father makes himself quite at home amongst them* [the Methodists] *and takes the Travelling Preacher's appointment very frequently.*" By their first spring in America, William is preaching for the church.

[Spring 1851]

My Dear Sister

I should very much like to see you again, you are not forgotten by me. The name of Emily is very frequently mentioned in the family. I wish you were amongst us scolding us once more. I would bear all the scolding in the world if I could but see you again. I suppose you are not married yet, give my love to John and tell him not to be afraid of the Yankees for he will make a very good one himself. I think he would like the Methodists a great deal better than he does there, my father makes himself quite at home amongst them and takes the Travelling Preacher's appointment very frequently.

The weather is very changeable here. Yesterday it was so hot that we were obliged to throw up the windows and put the fires out, and this evening it has become so cold that the windows are closed and a good fire in the stove. While I am writing, Mamma is sitting on the rocking chair, Edmund is making a ball, Mary is writing to Bertha, and Freddy and Bobby are building houses with wooden bricks. Although the weather is very changeable, it is very dry, for we have not had to dry the clothes before the fire more than once this winter. A beautiful Newfoundland dog higher than the table fathered himself upon us at the beginning of winter and has been with us ever since. He goes out and comes in with us and sleeps under Alfred and my bed.

I am ashamed to send this scribble for the writing is so bad, but the paper makes against me.

I remain your affectionate Brother

George

~ ~ ~

Letter #6 – Sister Mary to Emily

This letter from Mary (now fifteen years old) was in the same envelope as Ann's and George's. At age fifteen Mary is showing concern for Emily. "*My father's circumstances must have caused you a great deal of trouble...*" Mary (also calling the unpaid debts "*circumstances*") knows that in their departure the family has left Emily exposed to both the debts, and to the social censure of their community in England.

It is clear from this letter that Mary is aware of the debts. Mary then says, "*Refer as little as possible to the debts in your letters. It only makes* [Father] *low for he is not able to pay them at present, and I am afraid never will. It causes him much grief and he often says he had half a mind to go to California for the purpose of obtaining gold, to repay them.*"

William's conscience is bothering him at this early stage of migration. It is possible that William's original plan to go West when they migrated to America was with the idea of participating in the Gold Rush in California, which had peaked in the years 1848 and 1849. However, the family stopped in Troy in 1850 to rest, and stayed to settle.

[Spring 1851]

Dear Emily,

How much I should like to see you I cannot express; you may judge by your anxiety to see us. If we are ever privileged with each other's society again, we shall know better how to value the blessing. Alfred I suppose bears in mind his former little quarrels with you, for he rarely if ever crosses me at all. He is considered here by married ladies a very good looking young man. As to single ones, he never looks at them, and Mama says she hopes he never will. What think you? I am surprised to hear that your acquaintance with Taylors is at an end. I cannot think the cause. Why were you not more explicit? Do let me know in your next. We are not much surprised at Dr. Metson; for as you observe, we know the ----- . My father's circumstances must have caused you a great deal of trouble; refer as little as possible to the debts in your letters. It only makes him low for he is not able to pay them at present, and I am afraid never will. It causes him much grief and he often says he had half a mind to go to California for the purpose of obtaining gold, to return to England and pay them. Not that he would remain in England, for we all like America too well, as we can live very comfortably, but cannot save money. As to going to California, Mama is determined not to stir a [fig ?]. I think we should be driven to great extremities to leave Troy while she lives, for she is very fond of the place. Never mind troubling yourself about the things that Ma and I sent for, as we can do very well without them, and perhaps the money may be more useful to yourself. I am glad to hear that John's shop is so full of books. Give my love to him, and tell him I hope he will bring plenty of his with him when he comes to America.

I am dear sister,
Your affect,

Mary

Letter #7 – Ann to Emily

Ann writes Emily in May of 1851. Although the family has decided to stay in Troy, Ann asks Emily to lie on their behalf about their location, to make sure the creditors cannot continue to 'bother' them. Furthermore, Ann counsels deception about the preaching work that William wishes to take up.

Ann is up-front about the two lies, surmising that should any of the disgruntled people in England ("*malicious persons*") find out that William has taken up preaching again, they would disclose the facts behind his trans-Atlantic move. Ann recognizes that William would not be allowed to preach if people knew he had fled England owing money.

According to Ann, William joins her in asking Emily to conceal what he is doing in America.

Although the Cluetts have just given up the grocery store, Ann adds, "*It has answered one very good purpose, that of keeping us* [here] *'til we have established a charracter, which is worth a great deal in America.*" Ann recognizes the important social currency of establishing a good moral reputation, and she and William lie to achieve it.

About Washburne (a business associate or a creditor) she says, *"he has no power to trouble but he can annoy."* It appears that Ann sees the anger and ill feeling of those left unpaid as somehow undeserved by the Cluetts. Further, *"It is useless subjecting ourselves to annoyance* [meaning from the creditors] *to do no good. We cannot pay our debts and the Lord our judge knows it."*

However, she adds, *"If you should be fortunate to receive any money, give it to any of the creditors you think proper."* See Emmie Cadby Henry's recollections in Appendix D for her description of the strained financial state of her parents, Emily and John Cadby, in those early years.

Troy May 6 1851

My dear Child, I should not have written to you just now, but we expect to have to leave Troy toward the beginning of June. (Read your aunt's letter.) We had a letter yesterday from "Washbourne" expressing every confidence in your father's honesty and so on, of course he has no power to trouble, but he can annoy. Now I wish you to tell all enquirers that we are about moving, and never tell anyone (even when you know), where we are gone to. It is useless subjecting ourselves to annoyance to do no good. We cannot pay our debts, and the Lord who is our judge knows it. You will see by your aunt's letter that your father is about to go out as a Traveling Preacher. That you had better keep a secret too, for malicious persons may try to injure him. We have given up the store for want of money to carry it on. However, it has answered one very good purpose, that of keeping us in our place till we have established a charracter, which is worth a great deal in America. Your father had a situation offered to him of between 3 and 4 pounds per week, but did not understand book keeping, so was obliged to refuse it, and put up with one for the present at one pound five in a large cabinet maker's store. His employment is easy, but the hours are long. He goes at 7 A.M. and stays till 7 at night, comes home to his meals. If he does not go out as a Preacher, he will apply himself to bookkeeping, which they say he will learn in three months, and he has a friend here who will teach him free of expence. So you see my dear child our Heavenly Father is still mindful of us, feeding us with a Shepherd's care. I hope we shall all be more grateful to him for his great mercies manifested toward us.

I am glad you and your aunt are in earnest about eternal things. I wish you were here. You would soon be made an active useful character amongst us. Every one's zeal and abilities seem to be appreciated, and put into action, and there is plenty of work to do. I am sure you would be in your element. Your father is invited to preach at three different Churches, for the Traveling Preachers next Sunday. If we leave Troy Alfred wishes to remain, but unless we go somewhere near, I shall not leave him. The loss of one child is enough for me. If we do not go, there is a prospect after a while of sending something over now and then towards the debts. But we must leave all in the hands of God, who will, I am sure, cause all things to work together for our good. Make it as public as you like, or can, that we are about moving, but your father desires that you will not mention his preaching to any creature, but John, and your uncle and aunt Lewis, for we have enemies on that side of the water. If you should be fortunate to receive any money, give it to any of the creditors you think proper. The young lady you sent the parcel by did not come, but sent it by Express. It cost 1/sterling. Thank you for the Pamphlet. I can assure you it has been read with very great interest. I shall send you another letter when your father writes to your uncle. Till then my precious child, farewell, live near to God, and may every blessing attend to you and yours

prays your affectionate Mother

Ann Cluett

~ ~ ~

Letter #8 – Mary to Emily

Mary's letter here was in the same envelope with Ann's to Emily.

My dear Sister,

As John is about taking larger premises in New St. we have done expecting him to come to America especially as his friends are likely to make ----- agreeable. I am grieved they are on your account, but you must not think of feathering your nest in Birmingham. You asked to be informed how we are all employed here. Where to begin. My Father has little to do. He sits in his office parts of the day, and the other part he is in the store showing or selling furniture. Mama wakens in the morning between five and six o'clock, has her breakfast between six and seven, and sits sewing in bed till about eight, when she rises, takes a walk, and returns to cook the dinner. Then, after that, she has a nap and she and I generally take a long walk if she is well enough. Alfred has a situation in an Insurance Office, where he has three dollars a week. He goes at six in the morning and remains till eight at night with exception of meal times. He has very little writing to do for it would not suit his eyes. As for myself, I am girl of all work. I practise, but very little, not having a piano in the house. Father intends buying me one when he has an opportunity for I could earn a good living by teaching music, as teachers have twelve dollars a quarter for each pupil.

[No more exists of this letter]

Letter #9 – Ann to Emily

Troy August 20, 1851

My dear child

You say you always think it a long while before we answer your letters, now I can assure you we think the same by you. Before your Uncle's last letter came, we almost began to think we never should hear from any of you again. I am thankful to hear that you are well, are happy, and that you are likely so soon to have a comfortable home. But how I wish you were going to live near to us. I think it is too bad, but it cannot be helped. I must be resigned. I cannot hold out anything that will be likely to tempt John to give up a good business and come here. Therefore, with a full heart, I must wish you all the happiness a married life on that side the waters will afford. I like your dress and mantle much, but should not think they would look well worn together. Let me know generally what you wear, as I may the more easily picture your image to my mind's eye. Your ----- dress I like, it is light and pretty. What have you chosen for your wedding dress? I suppose something that will be useful to you afterwards.

I am not well, my appetite is bad, & I am very weak. When I came into this country first the air seemed to stimulate me so that my stomach would take anything, but now I have gone back to my old standing. I want another thorough change. Mr. McNulty, the Catholic priest came to see us the other day & invited me to his house for a while, for the benefit of my health, but I cannot bear travelling. He lives at Saratoga, a famous watering place, thirty miles from here, where great numbers resort during the summer for the benefit of the waters. There is an Inn there, the largest in the world, where more than 300 servants are kept! I should much like to see it.

I have had another letter from Mary, and she says she likes her situation first rate. She is, as you may say, quite the lady, but it will not last long, for I shall not be able to do without her. I told her I would try to do awhile. She said I must have a servant, and let Mary stay if I could, for they liked her very much.

The moskutoes have troubled us a good deal this last fortnight. They are small things, a very little larger than a flea, with long transparent wings, and their shrill hum never fails to waken us out of our sleep. They will bite either night or day.

I find I have left too much space between the lines on this side, so I will fill it up with rattle

[V.H.G. – Ann Cluett now turns the paper upside down, and begins to write between the lines of the first part of the letter!]

Alfred makes very little out learning ----- . He gets out of patience with it, and then hammers it, and makes it sound like a lot of bulls roaring. He is very much altered in his appearance, although he looked so juvenile in England, he is now taken to be 20 years of age. A lady inquired the other day after the health of his wife! He says he shall never rest now until he is married. He is particular in his dress, if he could afford it he would be the greatest Dandy in the place.

This year is a year for peaches, they are 8 cents per quart; apples, melons, and plums are plentiful. Potatoes are very cheap, but we do not eat many, seldom more than a quart a meal. Bread is cheaper than it was last year. Meat is dear if you buy regular joints, but you can buy a beaver [beef ?] heart for 4 cents that will be enough for all our dinners, and other things equally cheap, such as calves head, knuckle of veal, etc. But I cannot cook now like I could last year. I had used to cook 3 or 4 sorts of vegetables. And pies, and pudding too, but now I am seldom able. Frequently they are obliged to do with rice pudding, or bread and butter and coffee. Alfred met with a cask of grocers currants, weighing 130 lbs at 3 cents per lb, and plenty of those with rice and new milk makes very good pudding without eggs. When Mary was at home we were no better off, for she would rather starve than cook. I like it ----- well, with these stoves when I am able to do it. Mary will work herself almost to death to keep the house clean and keep things in order. But she will not cook. I wish you were here to give us a lift now and then. The name of the place where Mary is, is Chester; if you have a map of N.Y. State, you will find it north, joining Vermont State.

Your father has become a complete teetotaller, he says he is much better with drinking water. Indeed most of the Methodists here are teetotalers. I do not think I have ever been asked to take a glass of wine since I came to Troy. They will ask you to take a glass of milk.

Mr Ward is very kind, but he is looking through a telescope. You say you often wish you could have one peep at us. How often do I wish I could have one at you. I can take an imaginary peep of John in his shop. I fancy I sometimes see him busy recommending his books to his customers with a good grace, and a smile on his face.

[End of writing between the lines.]

Your father has been unwell with the diarrhea. It was brought on by eating apple pye and drinking a bason [?] of milk with it. He is now better, but it has prevented him from going to the Camp meeting. The children are all well, and as happy as possible. It is now the boys kite season, and they go most afternoons, when the lessons are done, to fly them on the hill. When there is a good wind they have fine fun, with now and then a good tumble head over heels on the grass. I go with them when I am well enough, and enjoy the scenery while they are playing. You say you have forgotten some of their birthdays. Edmund's is Oct 2, Freddy's May 18, Bobby's June 14. You say you always dream of Mary looking pale and wan. The reverse is the case, for she looks well and ruddy. I never dream of you, but you are crying, and it distresses me. I suppose it is owing to the impression the last glance at your countenance made on my mind. You were then crying, and I saw you through the window, as I sat in that nasty thing that hurried me away from the sight of my beloved child. Enough of this, I must drop the subject.

Aug 24 Your father has had another attack of bowel complaint, for a short time very severe. I was obliged to send for the doctor with all speed. I imprudently let him eat some apple pudding which brought it on again. We must be more cautious for the future. He is now much better, but it has made him very weak.

The boys are going to school again next week. They have had 5 weeks of vacation, and I have not so much missed Mary as I should have done, but I suppose I must keep George at home in a morning. I had an application this week for him to go to learn the drapery business, it is at the store where I deal. I had not thought of putting him to that business, but he seems inclined to go and try. It may do as any other because a steady, persevering young man in this country has so many chances of going into partnership. I meant to have kept [him] at school till next spring but it is not much consequence, for he is not very fond of learning.

I have just seen a local Preacher, an English man who has been at the Camp meeting and he says they had a most extraordinary time. The presence of God was powerfully felt amongst them. Alfred's Class Teacher who is also English was there, and he is most opposed to noise & excitement, and is also a shy & diffident man. Well the Power came down upon him, and he was determined to keep it in, and the consequence was that he fell down in strong convulsions. Another pious, good man was so overpowered that he fell upon his knees, and remained there about four hours weeping, and rejoicing. Surely this is the Work of God; I wish we had more of it. I hope my dear Emily you are growing in grace and in the love and knowledge of God. I pray earnestly for you, that you may be real Christian. Do not fail to pray for me, that I may be able to do, and suffer, the will of God.

Alfred & George would have written this time, but there is not room, so you must be satisfied with their best love. You say nothing about the Taylors. Is Mr. T. still living? How is Mrs. Ludlow? And any old friend you think of write. Just mention. Give my love to John. Tell him not to forget me. I should have written to him, but there is not room. Farewell my dear child.

The Lord bless you prays your affectionate Mother

A Cluett

I have just this minute seen a beautiful chariot drawn by ten pairs of horses.

How does Bertha like her situation, and what is her salary? Tell me all about your new dwelling.

Letter #10 – Father William to daughter Emily

William writes Emily with news and business questions; he remarks on her upcoming marriage and wishes her well.

Troy Sep 4th 1851

My Dear Emily,

I learn from Dr. Skilton that his son has seen you, therefore conclude that you recd. my last short note. I suppose it gave you pleasure to see & speak to one who has so recently seen & spoken to us.

I too, shall be glad for the same reason, to see him again. As to the time when we shall all meet again, I see no chance of determining at present. It must be left to the ordering of Him who "doeth all things well". As it regards our return to England, that may regarded as an event, if not impossible, yet highly improbable; inasmuch as without considerable funds, it would be more than folly to return where everything is so expensive; & I am not sure that we should like to remain even if we could return tomorrow. The longer people live in this country, the better they like it. The prospect is much brighter here for the children than it is in England. In fact, if we possessed large means, or should we at some future time be in possession of such means, it would be unwise to leave America, for the simple reason that all the comforts & conveniences of England can be obtained here for far less cost. If our friends were around us, we should feel about as much at home as in any place where we have resided. We are now beginning to know the people, & the people to know us. It is [necessary ?] for a person to reside in America for some time, (if he comes as we came, perfect strangers), before he can hope for any great success in his undertakings, but every steady & industrious person is sure to succeed finally.

Dr. Skilton tells us his son writes that [Mr. Cope ?] is coming in the early part of the month. If so, he will leave Birm. [Birmingham] before you get this, but I begin to entertain doubts about his coming at all, though I think he would be glad to get away from the strife & --------- --------------- church. If you can procure 2 or 3 secondhand copies of the Wesleyan Times, published during the sittings of the Conference, we should be glad to receive them, as we know very little of what is going on, but understand there is much confusion. Well, I am glad to be removed from the excitement & [uproar?] I thought I should be prepared to give you a full & particular account of an American Camp Meeting in this letter, but Mr. Clapp went on business to New York & did not return in time for me to go. I wish you were amongst us here, you would like Troy Methodism better than Birmg'm. Methodism. We have not so many "stuck up" people here. A man is admired by his mind & conduct rather than the amount of his dollars.

Our summer has been a most delightful one. We have not had more than 4 or 5 hot days, but the falling leaves are indicating the approach of a cooler season, though we look for the next 2 months to be about as delightful as any part of the year. I wish I could send you a part of the delicious peaches, & a few of the melons of which we have such an abundance. You will have to live in America to enjoy fully the luxury of a ripe peach on a warm day. We are all of us rather careful of eating fruit of any kind, as we have the fear of the Bowell complaint before our eyes. With all my care, I got a sharp attack of it last week, but it is passed off fairly well. People often say, that those who take the greatest care are most liable to do it, & I am inclined to believe so. I suppose your Mama has told you all the news about Mary, Alfred, & the rest of the Children, therefore I need not say anything, only just tell you that they grow so fast that if you don't make all haste to pay us a visit, you will not be likely to know them when you do come. Alfred seems likely to be a [stiff ?] little fellow of 6 feet or upwards.

If we remain in Troy, as it appears likely we shall do, we intend to use some efforts to obtain a cottage of our own next Spring. This is a far less difficult matter to accomplish than you would imagine.

Your Mama says she will not be satisfied till we have a place to call "our own". We have lived too long in England to feel quite satisfied with anything less than "a house to ourselves".

I thought I had forwarded you with Armson's a/c [account]. I now give it to you in full. If Mr. Rowley should require his Baptismal name, your Uncle Radnale can give it to you. I think he will pay as soon as Mr. Rowley writes him. He is Carpenter & Builder at -----

C ----- is in circumstances to be able to pay at once.

Mr. Armson
To W.C. Dr. [debtor]

To Registry 300 Bills of Sale of Houses	17..0
" Man 2 days posting D [ditto]	8..0
" 3 advertisements in Wolverhampton paper	19..0
" 2 " Birmingham D [ditto]	15..6
" attending sale	1..1..0
	4..0..6

John will copy this Bill for you,

I owed something to Mr. Wallos, the printer. Have you ever had his a/c? or has it been paid? I think of many enquiries which I wish to make, but they do not occur to me at the right time. I suppose before you write again you will have exchanged your single for a married life. I conclude, under all incumstances [circumstances ?], that it is the best thing you can do. Well, I pray God, my dear Emily, that you may never feel ----- regret for having taken such a life, than I have felt during that many ----- disappointments & happiness of upwards 20 years. If a married life has trials peculiar to itself, it has also its peculiar pleasures. I have always been of opinion that outside the [wall ?] of matrimony, neither man nor woman knows anything about the sweets of "HOME". I thought of writing a much longer letter, but your Mamma is ----- with me to send it off, so I suppose I must come to a conclusion. Be sure to write us again as soon as you can. You have more time (I presume) than I have. I am obliged to write a bit; I leave the rest to another opportunity. Give my best respect to all inquiring friends. Should dearly like to pay you a flying visit, but "Old Jordan rolls between". Farewell, my Dear Emily. That God would bless you with His [cherished ?] blessings is the prayer of your affectionate father.

W.C.

P.S. I think you say in your last letter that Mr. Cope was expecting one from me. I wrote him one a long time since & have been ----- at not having heard from him again. Perhaps he has not rec'd. my last.

Address your next letter to
W. Cluett
care of Mr. N. Clapp
Box 54, Post Office
Troy, N.Y.
America

~ ~ ~

Letter #11 – William to son-in-law John

This letter, from William to son-in-law John, was mailed with the preceding letter.

Troy Sep 4th 1851

Dear John,

It affords me great pleasure to hear your business is in a flourishing state. If you can make plenty of purchases such as those referred to in you last letter, I see nothing to prevent your success. Your [enumerations ?] of the Books and prices make my mouth water. I fear I shall never be quite at home till I am in the Book trade again. I very much regret having sold so many of my own before I left Eng. I have fewer books than I have had for the last 20 years, & never in the whole [course ?] of that period did I need them so much as at present. I have an intelligent congregation to address every Sunday in 2 churches alternately, consequently am obliged to do considerably in the way [of study ?]. How I wish the lot you got from Mr. Davis could be transported to 168 fifth st. [where the Cluetts were living at the time] at 100 percent profit, as well as the lot containing the ----- . The latter would be a great prize to me, as I have never seen one in the country. Every time I think about ----- I am vexed with having parted with it. Hundreds of books are amazingly cheap here, but many of them are of the kind that I do not want. I picked up in the ----- the other day a copy of James' last work "The Fate" which is published here at half a dollar only & I suppose the English price is 1/11/6. Nearly all the expensive English ----- Tales are published here complete for about 1/- or 2/-

each; but Theological Works are not cheap. If I could visit New St. with the necessary funds, I should soon make some empty spaces in your shelves, but as there is little possibility of that, I must patiently want the opportunity of supplying myself in some other Way.

I have not yet been able to visit New York. I am very anxious to do so as I continue to hear from various quarters that it is a [first rate ?] place for the Book trade. I shall try to visit it before I write again. I would advise you to scrape together & save all you can, & in --------------- to this keep your expenses as low as possible. If a change for the worse should come over your business at a future time, & you should begin to think of America as your future home, remember that money is worth considerably more, & consequently will accomplish more than it will in England. I have met with so many fluctuations at home that I have no confidence in business remaining good for any length of time. The best thing is to make hay while the sun shines. Money gets money very fast in this country and therefore the man of money soon becomes rich. A man who was formerly in a Book store adjoining our place commenced for himself last Autumn & I am informed on good authority that he is doing well, although I doubt it – still the Books in his store would fill 4 tea chests! I have enclosed ------------------- You will oblige me by putting in an envelope & sending it to him.

Remember me kindly to your Father, Mother, & Sister,

And believe me to be, dr [dear] John
Your truly & affect

W.C.

Letter #12 – Mary to Emily

Mary is now teaching music, and becomes another busy Cluett family earner in Troy.

Troy, N.Y. [Oct., 1852]

My dearest Emily,

I suppose by this time that you have almost given up all hope of ever hearing from us again; I really feel ashamed of our conduct but I hope we shall be so severely censured by you when you find by reading Mama's letter, that our silence has been unavoidable. Well now I will try to pen a few remarks and presume to give them the name of letter. I must confess I feel unequal to the task and if it is rather a short one you will please excuse me for I am at present without a servant; my last left me very unceremoniously a few days since, and the one we have engaged cannot come to us for a week or so. My business increases rapidly. I have raised my charge to eight dollars per quarter, as I can get more respectable scholars at that price. I have three pupils out of one family. Ah Emily! You will laugh when you hear of me as a public character; I should think you ought to feel proud of your little sister who used to cause you so much trouble but enough of this rattle. Oh pardon me I forgot to say that one of my pupils is a professor in a large institute for young gentlemen.

Oct. 20th. I do not know when I shall be able to finish my letter. I have so many interruptions. For three successive evenings I have thought of sitting down and writing but have been disturbed by visitors. The weather here has been exceedingly beautiful for some time, and often have I wished for your company while a party of us have been taking a stroll by moonlight. And now I come to our spiritual affairs. I am happy to inform you that George has join'd the church and meets in the same class as Alfred. He is now a very different boy to what he formerly was; I do think everybody loves him. Alfred enjoys much religion in his soul, I believe he has been enabled to give himself entirely to the Lord. Bro Griffin, our boarder, experienced sanctification a few weeks since, and is a pattern of godliness to us. I also feel that I am cleansed from all sin through the blood of the Lamb, and rejoice in the expectation of "Seeing Jesus as he is."

While I am writing, my Father is resting himself on the sofa, Mama is mending stockings, Alfred is composing at the piano, and the four boys in company with several others are holding a prayer-meeting in an upper room by themselves. It is their practice to have one of these meetings a week, and I think they will be the means of doing some little good. Methinks I hear you say "What a happy family!" I trust we may ever remain so. This evening we received John's catalogue, it is indeed a pretty one. I am glad to hear of your good health and prosperity, and of little Johnny's baptism. How I wish I could in some way see my dear little

[no more of this letter exists]

[Mary]

Letter #13 – Mary to Emily

By November 1852, Mary is attending Sabbath School along with her siblings: *"I believe I have before told you that the richest in this country attend Sabbath School,"* an indication that the Cluetts wanted to associate with those who are well-off. In the minds of Troy society, and the Cluett family, wealth is equated with good moral station.

Troy [Nov 1852]

My dear Sister

will, I have no doubt, think I have forgotten her, but my long silence has not proceeded from not desiring to write to the Sister I so dearly love, but from want of time. This is the first opportunity I have had, and even now I am writing while the children finish their tea. I read your last with mingled feelings of pleasure and pain; my heart was filled with gratitude to my God for delivering you in so great an hour of need. Truly the Lord is good to those who fear Him. I had not conceived it possible for you to suffer so much. I guess were there no other obstacle, the rehearsal of such suffering would deter me from removing in to the state of Matrimony. For the last few weeks, my time has been entirely engaged, as I am sorry to say Mama has had an unusually severe attack of illness; she has been confined to her bed for nearly four weeks, but is now far recover'd as to be able to leave her room, which is a great blessing. Her sickness has risen from her old disease, debilitated stomach.

Another thing that has engaged our minds, and employed our time, was an Exhibition of the Sabbath school connected with Ida Hill Church. We all belong to it. Alfred and I are teachers, and the rest are scholars. (I believe I have before told you that the richest in this country attend Sabbath School;) and as we furnished much of our English music, we all took a part in the performances. The stage for the school was erected close by the pulpit, from one side of the church to the other; the exercises for the evening were dialogues, sacred music, and pieces spoken by the children. We had the church crowded to excess. And now I will proceed to tell you what we did to help the Exhibition. After a class of girls had been questioned about the women of the bible as far as Miriam, the choir sang "Sound the Loud Timbrel", and George and I and a young man sung the trio in it. Then Alfred, I, and two more sung a quartette, "Love God"; George sung a beautiful piece, "My Mother's Bible" alone, and spoke a dialogue with Orville Howland. Edmund, Freddy, and Robert sung "Oh ye Sun and Moon", which was never heard here before. Edmund took the alto, and the two others, the air. I believe that piece carried the day. Then Robert sung all alone, "Great God, and will Thou condescend" and afterward played it on a beautiful little flute. So you see we have had enough to think about.

Dec. 1st. I have been obliged to discontinue my letter, as since writing the foregoing, I have had the Scarlet Fever. The complaint set in rather severely but on the 2nd day from the commencement, I was advised to be packed in a wet sheet, with a weight upon me heavier than a feather bed and you will be surprised to hear that such a process broke up the fever immediately. I am now rapidly improving, though still very weak, as you will perceive by my handwriting. You will please excuse such scribble.

And now I have to tell you some good news. For many months past we have held a young people's prayermeeting every Wednesday evening. You cannot conceive what large and happy meetings we have; it would rejoice your heart if you could attend them with us, and enjoy great and precious privileges. Oh that I could be more thankful for them! Respecting our family they are well; Edmund and Fred continue at school, and I believe are much beloved by their master, and Bob studies at home. I would like when you next write, to tell us what you all wear (my dear little nephew included). I have for winter a green drawn bonnet, white border and strings, for best, and quilted blue satin bonnet hood for everyday, a new shawl, a green de laine dress, and a drab merino (which I had made for the Celebration) made plain flowing sleeves, trimm'ed with black velvet, white undersleeves, an insertion habit shirt, a worked linen collar, and a pink bow. This was my dress on that celebration night. Mama was quite anxious to write, but does not feel quite equal to the task, having had so much to think about during my illness. And as to coming back to England, that I think we shall never do. We have become so attach'd to this country that if we return to England, it will simply be a visit to our dear friends. I have thought it next to an impossibility for an adopted Mother, to be as kind as an own Mother, but I have proved it otherwise for I am sure our adopted country has behaved better to us than our Mother country would ever do except we lived in affluence. Please give my kind love to Aunt & Uncle Lewis, Bertha, big John, middle John and little John, Mr. and Mrs. Cadby. Tell John, I rejoice that his business is so much increased and that the dear baby is so good. When shall I see you all again? I think I could endure anything almost, if I might see you. Though there is no sign of us meeting yet, let us often meet at a throne of grace, and so live, as finally to meet in heaven.

Good bye dear Emily for the present may you abound in every good word and work is the prayer of

Your sincerely affectionate

Mary

All the family send their kindest love to all. Freddy and Bob have been busy practicing writing for some time to send you a letter.

~ ~ ~

Letter #14 – Ann to Emily

V.H.G. – The top and bottom margins of the previous letter are filled with the following note from Ann Cluett.

My dear child, I have a great deal to say to you but am not able to write this time. I long to see you now more that I ever did and if I had [known] things would have turned out as they have, I never would have left England. I mean as regards yourself. There appears no sign of you or your aunt coming here. I cannot come to you, if would, I am not able. Please let us know how the Grinsells are doing, and Cope's when you hear. I hope your uncle and aunt Lewis are better. We are looking out for a letter from them. How does your cousin John behave himself now?

[Ann]

Letter #15 – Brother Alfred to Emily

Sixteen months have passed. In this animated letter from Alfred, he tells Emily that he has joined the Collar business; he also gives lively descriptions of his siblings. Alfred is twenty years old when he writes.

Troy, N.Y. March 1/54 [1854]

My very dear sister Emily,

I suppose you are ready for another letter from me. I am quite willing that you should have one, but really I don't know how to fill this sheet of paper with matter sufficiently interesting to repay the trouble of reading, but I will tell you all about myself, my prospects, experience &c [etc] so that you can know what Alfred is doing and how the world uses him. In the first place I am what is called here a Linen Dealer but vulgarly denominated a Collar Maker. I am now entering upon my third year at the business, and I think it is very probable it will be my permanent trade. My salary is 400 Dollars about £1.11 a week, you must know that I can live very comfortably on that and save a little also. Have you ever seen a "stitching machine"? We have in Troy upwards of 300 of them, and they have worked quite a revolution in the Collar trade. They stitch much finer than they can be done by hand. Each machine if in good order will stitch 40 Doz per day. We have ten of them at work at my establishment.

I think that in almost every letter I sent to England I have said something in praise of my adopted country. Well — I wish you to know that my sentiments are unchanged and are every year becoming more deeply fixed. I am more an American now than I ever was, and shall never be a royalist again as long as I live, this is the place for a Young Man, he can be Man here if he likes and to every one there is a straight road to comfort and plenty. I wish you to understand that I have made a start. And it is now "Alfred Cluett versus the World". What do you think of my chance. Am I going to win the day? Doubtless you recollect the old Proverb. When you are in Rome, you must do as the Romans do, and when in Turkey, do as the Turkies do. Now I am in America I must do as the Yankees do, but I am pretty sure I can do better than some of them. Mary is now quite a professor and is busy as a bee. Her Pupils keep her on the move, and she puts forth every effort to increase her business. She advertises, and circulates her cards, and finds many new friends.

George is one of the Boys. Sports a fancy knitted coat with velvet collar, silver watch and fixings, standing collar and all the latest Yankee improvements. He gets good wages now and is in a great hurry to be somebody. Edmund is equal to any Yankee of his size, and moreover is not afraid of his shadow. He pines for a watch and sighs for a standing collar, and earnestly desires, yea thirsts, to be numbered with the brightest specimens of the human family.

Frederick (late Freddy) possesses all the prognostications of genius, in the highest degree. High forehead, pale face, large blue eyes, and a retiring disposition. He performs on the Piano very creditably and has great knowledge of music. He has progressed finely in his studies and is on the high road to science [success ?].

Robert ----- develops curiously. I really can not make up my mind as to what he is or what he will be. His stature will never be exceeding great and if he grows at all --- it is sideways. But however small he is --- or may be, he possesses self confidence enough for a Brobdingnagian [V.H.G.: an inhabitant of a country in "Gullivers Travels"].

He will certainly make his way through the World if he is permitted to stay long enough in it. Thus endeth the description of the children of Mr and Mrs Cluett — and the rest of their acts are they not written and deposited in the same envelope that contains my epistle.

I am glad to hear that you and your family are all doing so well and I want you to see that all my nephews and nieces have a good musical education, the next boy that comes along in the course of events, I want you to name him after me, I think there should be at least two J.W. Alfreds in the world. I hope you and my very excellent brother John will take the matter into consideration.

I want John to write me a letter and tell me all about matters and things, and the book trade in general. I suppose he is very busy but if he does not write me soon I shall cut his acquaintance. Which will be a serious matter for him.

I shall now conclude with a few lines for yourself expressly, take care of number one, and let not your heart be troubled, you are prospering on your side of the Atlantic and we on ours. I shall (if things go well with me) meet you on your own ground, in the course of a few years, and we will have a good time of it. ---so don't forget

Your Affectionate Brother

J.W. Alfred Cluett

Letter #16 – Ann to Emily

In this letter from Ann we hear that *"George has gone to be with Alfred"* in the collar business. Although George later had greater leadership in the collar companies than did Alfred, Alfred was the first to enter the business.

Troy March 4, 1855

My Dear Child

We received your long long expected but very welcome letter 15 days after date and I have a great mind to give you a good reprimand for keeping us so long without it. Every time a ------came in we were all on the tip toe of expectation and greatly disappointed when nothing came. At length I became exceedingly uneasy fearing some of you were ill, or that something bad had happened. Well I suppose I must forgive you (if you will promise never to do so again) on the [plea ?] of your multiplied engagements. I know your family, though small, require great attention. How I lament that you are not near to us that we may share in your anxieties and pleasures. Your dear little children must be now very interesting. Their aunt and uncles are frequently talking about them, and when they see a little girl or boy, they say "I wonder whether that is anything like one of Emily's". A short time ago we had a little boy from the country to stay a few days with us, and his funny sayings amused them so much that they have become more anxious than ever to see their little nephew and niece. Nothing on earth would give us all so much pleasure as to have you to live where we could see you every day. Will that ever be the case? Yes, it must be, I will never give up while life lasts. If I were to be assured that I should never see you again, I should go mourning all my days.

My health has been tolerably well this winter, better than it had been for two or three winters past. I generally spend my mornings in the kitchen helping Bridget, then in the afternoon if it is warm enough, I go for a short walk, and if not, I sit to my sewing for the rest of the day, for I have always plenty to do. You say in your last that your aunt surmised that you had said something to hurt my feelings, It was quite a mistake, and I am at a loss to know what could have given rise to the idea. No, my dear child has never said, or done anything to grieve me for the last ten years.

March 22. We received your welcome letters the day before yesterday, and were very sorry to hear that your little Mary had been so ill. The time of teething is a very troublesome time. I wish you had not told us that she had a relapse just before you sealed your letter. I shall be anxious about you till I hear again from you. I think if you were here I would be as fond of your little birds as I was of my own. How glad I should be if I was where I could relieve you of your anxiety about them. If you had lived in this country you would not have been allowed to sit nursing your baby night & day alternately for two weeks with your sister-in-law. No, you would have had all your near neighbors in sympathizing with you, and rendering you all the assistance in their power night and day. The nearest friends of the patient are kept as much as possible out of the room, and relieved of all fatigue, the anxiety being sufficient for them to bear. It is an excellent practice – one worthy of imitation in all countries.

I am thankful to hear that you were both resigned to the will of God when you thought your little darling would be taken from you. It affords me great comfort, and I hope before this time she is restarted to perfect health. I am very glad too that John is doing so well in his business. Tell him he must not exert himself too much, but use moderation. He has but one life to him. It does me good however to hear that he is preparing for the life to come.

April 3. We received a letter from your Uncle Lewis a few days ago, and were glad to hear that your little Mary is better. Your aunt says she is the sweetest little creature she ever saw, indeed that both your children are beautiful and lovely. She says she is extremely fond of them, and wishes I could see them. Alas, I wish so too, but I see no prospect of it at present. Still, we know not what is in the future.

To night is the prayer meeting, and your father, Mary, Alfred and George have gone there. Edmund, Freddy, and I are in the parlour together. Robert has gone to bed, and Bridget is in the kitchen ironing. Robert is the most undaunted customer I ever met with. His motto is "Where there is a will there is a way". If he is in pursuit of an object, impediments discourage him not, but rather stimulate him to greater perseverance. He has a great spirit, and perhaps it will be well for him, for his body will be very short. He is a great trader in his way. I do not know how many [sleighs ?] he has bought and sold this winter. He bargains and exchanges with the boys. I do not mean to say he always does it to profit, but he must be trading even if he is loser. If we want anything repaired, Robert is the one to apply to, and what he cannot do himself, he will take to a coachmaker or Blacksmith, and they will do it for him free of cash. Freddy tells him he is completely ashamed of him and will not own him as a brother, but we tell Freddy that while he is sitting at the Piano waiting for pupils, Robert will be off gathering the "Fin" together in heaps. Edmund is nearly fifteen years old, and it is time to put him to some business, but like most of the others, he is very small of his age. I do not know yet what we shall put him to learn. He goes to school at present, and is making pretty good progress. George has left his situation and has gone to be with Alfred. He wrote a letter to his cousin John in the last packet, but it was not even acknowledged. He is very much offended and says he will not write to any of you again until he has a letter.

Your sister's health has not been so good this winter as it used to be. She thinks her business does not suit her health so well as hard work. She has too much sitting down. Sometimes she thinks of giving up a part of it and keeping no girl, that she might have more exercise, but I do not think that would answer. However, some alteration must be made, for her health is not so good since she has devoted her time to music.

I hope my dear child your health is better. Do take care of yourself and get out all you can into the fresh air. And let me beg of you not to be anxious about us or lament because we are so far apart, we shall meet again. Yes, I hope in this world. We are not so far apart after all, two weeks would bring us together. [Cheer up ?] you have everything to make you comfortable and happy, and that affords me great consolation. Your aunt & uncle speak in high terms of your establishment, your husband, and your children, and as to yourself she says you dress like a little queen.

I need not tell you about your father's business, as he has told John all about it. However, I would just remark that I think it will ultimately answer well, as we draw little or nothing out to keep house with; what Mary & the boys get being nearly sufficient. Then his partner has never drawn anything out yet. He is an energetic business man and I think they will work together very well.

When you write again (which I hope will be soon) send word whether you have heard anything about Mr. Cope, it will interest us much. I never thought he would like Australia. It is no trifle to go into a new country; coming to Troy is a very different thing, that seems little more than going from London to Liverpool. We have every accommodation here the same as we had in Birmingham.

I must now conclude with my best to you and John, and a great many kisses for the dear little "birds". Give my kind love to your uncle & aunt & tell them we shall write soon. Good bye my dear child, and I pray that the Lord may be with you, and keep you to the day of redemption.

[Ann Cluett]

Letter #17 – Mary to Emily

In April of 1855, Mary tells Emily of a great religious revival, particularly among young people. While the Cluetts are all heavily involved in music in Troy, the religious focus is yet more important.

"But you must not think that Music attracts all our attention. Oh no! Religion I believe has been the all absorbing theme with many, very many. We have had a gracious revival throughout the city. Presbyterians, Baptists, Methodists, all have had their minds eye centered on one object; that of saving souls."

Their religious passion is powerful and sincere.

Troy April 14th 1855

My dear Sister,

It is now Saturday morn and as I have an hour to spare, I will tell you a little about matters and things connected with us. It is about ½ past 7 o'clock. Mama is dressing to go out. Bridget is eating breakfast. Father, Alfred, and George are gone to the store and the boys are at play. When your last letter arrived I was not at home; I was visiting about 35 miles distant and was absent nearly a fortnight. I think I never before enjoyed a visit so much. I became acquainted with most of the Methodists in that village. Of course I had an opportunity of doing so as I was staying with a Methodist Minister's family who were stationed in Troy 2 years since. This conference he is going to locate and become Principal of a boarding school about three miles from here. His sister-in-law whose age is 30 or upwards, boarded with me this winter, preparing herself for a teacher of Music. She is now teaching in the above school which I am glad of, as she seems like a Sister to me. In [fact] she has a place in my affection next to you. I wish you were acquainted with Miss Smith. Mama likes her better than any young lady she knows.

Everything in this city is very dull. Provisions are high, business is bad, and I find that I have to participate, though much against my will, in the general dulness of trade. Yet we are much engaged in music. Edmund has been taking lessons on the Violin. Alfred devotes his spare time to the Piano. Fred is now engaged every evening in playing for a choir who are preparing for an "Old Folks" Concert which will take place in a week or two. Alfred, George and myself belong to the "Troy Musical Institute", an association which is only for gentlemen, is two dollars and half a dollar besides. Ladies are free from all payment whatever. We meet every Monday and Friday evening and I can assure we go through some difficult music. We have given two concerts, the first one, given about two months since, was "Hayden's Seasons". The Hall which was very large was so full that many had to return home without being able to gain entrance. It was so good we had to repeat it. We gave another last Tuesday, "Orotorio of David", to a very large audience, and I see by the papers that the public desire its repetition. We are now practicing on " ----- or Hymn to Liberty" composed by our Musical Director, which promises to go off well. Concerts are not considered here in the same light as in England, at least such as our's. Ministers and members of the different churches attend them. On Sabbaths we have to divide our services between two churches for, as we had for a length of time been petitioned by the Minister and people of the first M E [Methodist Episcopal] church in Troy to take seats in their choir, we proposed to sit with them once every Sunday on condition that we should have the use of the organ one evening in the week, to which proposition they gladly assented, saying that I might have the use of the organ whenever I pleased morning, noon, or night. I think it will be an advantage to me ultimately.

But you must not think that Music attracts all our attention. Oh no! Religion I believe has been the all absorbing theme with many, very many. We have had a gracious revival throughout the city. Presbyterians, Baptists, Methodists, all have had their minds eye centered on one object; that of saving souls. And bless the Lord their labors have not been in vain. There has been a great awakening amongst the young people, consequently, balls [halls ?] and such places of amusement have not been very popular here of late. Several of my pupils have sought the Lord and can now rejoice in the sense of their acceptance with God. This is what I have longed looked for and I pray that while I instruct them in music I may be enabled to instruct them in the way to Christ. A few days ago Mama had been doing a little shopping with a young man a friend of ours when followed her down the shop to the door, when he said, "Mrs. Cluett, you were talking to me the other day about becoming pious, and I followed your advice and now I am a Christian. I thought you would be glad to hear it. Oh I am so happy." That is genuine is it not? You must tell me in your next how Dr. Metson's class goes on. Does he ever ask about me?

In three weeks we shall move to a very pleasant house. It is in the city, but on a high rock far above the street and is so surrounded by peach and plumb trees that it seems quite like the country. It contains a good kitchen, dining room, two parlours, and eight bedrooms, rent 250 dollars per annum. We shall let 3 or 4 rooms for $65 or $70 and be able to keep one boarder. We have two boarders now but they will both join the Conference next month at which time we expect to have Proff Green. I do dread moving very much we move so often. We should not have done this year had there been any water attached to the house we now occupy. Conference commences on the ninth of May when I hope to be settled, as I am anxious to attend these sittings.

I often build castles in air and think about coming over to see you. I often rather envy sisters when I see them visit their sister's families. Polly must be a nice little girl. How I would like to see her. I am going to write to John on the next page so I must close with a great deal of love to Johnny, Polly, and all the rest of friends.

Keep a good share for yourself. I am Dear Sister,
yours as ever

Mary

~ ~ ~

Letter #18 – Mary to John

Mary also encloses a letter to brother-in-law John in this envelope.

My dear Brother John,

I suppose you are such a tradesman now that if I write to you I must not expect a letter in reply. I am very glad to hear of you doing such a good business, but I am really afraid that as long as it continues so, we shall not be able to see you on this side of the great deep, and I am so selfish as to want you here business or no business. What a pleasant thing it would be for us all to be together once more, and I think it would be funny enough to see you in the capacity of a Husband and Father; such a [shifting ?] as you used to be. Oh how things do change! You can tell Emily I think she was very fortunate in getting you when she did, for I am nineteen and can find nobody to suit me. Now you must be very sober when I tell you a story. A few weeks ago Father brought home a letter and looked so roguish that I knew something was in the wind. He handed it to Ma and Affie [Alfie?] and when I asked to see it he said it was not written to me. However I managed to catch a peek at it and sure enough it was written to Ma and Father but it very closely concerned me. The writer was a young man about entering the Ministry, 25 years of age and very nearly six feet high. He is good looking and a nice man but as I cannot be spared from home and I should not like such a tall man I told Father to answer in the negative. I fancy I see you laughing, well have your laugh out. Emily had a better chance for leaving home than I ever can have, so you see if I do not live to be an "Old Maid". I believe I have told all the news now. You will perceive this writing is bad but I cannot do better my hand shakes so. Give Johnny and Polly many kisses from me and tell me a great deal of news when you write. You must remember to take great care of your dear Wife. Aunt Lewis says she looks nicely. I am glad of it, and when I see you I will tell you how thankful I am to you.

Your very loving Sister,

Mary

Letter #19 – Mary to Emily

By 1856, they move from a house that had no water to a pleasant house high on a hill with fruit trees, two parlours and eight bedrooms, and they will have one boarder. Their new rent is $250 per year. And, while they make their own clothes and still "*are as saving as possible*", by this time the family is doing well and is now able to improve their lives with some extras.

Mary describes some of their new clothes, a new carpet, and new books bought by their father for the family library, succumbing to family pressure to buy books other than theological works.

Troy, N.Y. April 29, 1856

My dear Sister Emily,

Having taken my seat before my writing desk for the purpose of writing to you, I scarcely know with what subject to commence with. If I could only see you I am sure there would be no lack of matter on which to converse, but then writing is so different. I wish you could view our garden all round the house. It is laid out in front in the English style, in circles and half circles, with grass round them, and flowers in the middle. Mamma planned it herself and the younger boys dug it. Certainly it looks nicer than most gardens round Troy. I have never known Ma to be in better or so good health since the accident, as she has been for many months past. This is indeed a great mercy, and I sometimes fear that I am not sufficiently grateful for it. This morning she was up before I was out of bed, (a little before six o'clock).

You say you do not think they boys have at all improved during the six years absence from you. I think they have very much. George will in a few years if all is well, be quite a handsome man, and as good as he will be handsome. He and Alfred are very good boys, are very attentive to me, and dutiful to Mamma. I should not object to having five more brothers, if they could be similar to those I have.

I suppose I must keep you "posted up" as is the American's phrase, on our music. Since our Concert, we have done little indeed in Singing. I became so worn out by it, that I had to give it up and have scarcely recommenced yet, and of course the boys could not sing without me, so they have had to be content with Instrumental Music. I still give Robert Piano lessons. He likes it, but he cannot endure to practise an hour and half a day which Mama is very particular in having him do. He does not apply himself like Freddy.

It is the custom here every year, to go through the house from top to bottom whitewashing cleaning paint, taking up carpets, etc. We have almost finished except varnishing a few chairs. The green carpet that we brought with us that has lasted us on the sitting room ever since we came here is pretty well worn, so we bought another for the back parlour and put the green one on Mama's bedroom a nice larger room over the parlour. Father has also replenished our library. We used to teaze him about having no books but sermons and other theological works, so he at last made up his mind to fill his large bookcase with books suitable for all; most assuredly a good collection. When it was completed we thought we ought to give him a vote of thanks. I spend all my spare time in good reading. By spare time I mean all my time that is not spent in music for we have very little sewing just now, having made all the spring clothes. I have nothing new except a straw bonnet hemmed with blue and drab ribbon with white lining and border with a few little flowers interspersed. Mama has a new bonnet made of drab silk made quite plane, trimmed with the same mixed with lace, and pink ribbon in the border. It was my make. She has too, a new silk dress with a dark blue silk stripe across it. I want her to have a shawl but she thinks she does not need it. We make all our clothes, bonnets, mantles, all. And we are as saving as possible.

May 1st. As I have very little news to send, and as you would not be interested were I to tell you about anything not connected with our family I hardly know what to say. Today, as we have already informed you, is general moving day. The city presents a curious scene; wagons moving along the streets, filled with furniture. The blacks with their whitewashing buckets, and brushes altogether. This seems the busiest day in all the year. Father opens his new store today, with the Piano Salon upstairs. He came home last night very tired, and I was afraid he was going to be ill, but he rose this morning feeling quite well. Edmund also spent the day in the old store packing up; he is a help to Father; in fact he could not get along without him.

We often joke Alfred and George about two young ladies, of great respectability, to whom they are very attentive. They all meet in the same class, and of course the boys have to escort them home afterwards. It seems to be an understood affair by the community, who believe that Alfred is engaged to Mary, who is near my own age, and George to Sarah who is sixteen but it is nothing, it serves us to plague them about. Alfred I think has no idea of leaving home, but George is more fond of the ladies, and I guess as soon as he is old enough he will have a wife. It does not seem probable that I shall lead in your steps as far as taking so much care on my shoulders is concerned. I never saw any man yet that suited me. Some nights since a lady brought her brother-in-law to see me. He looks quite a gentleman, has some money, but is too quiet and too old, being over thirty, so you see I have no chance and shall have, oh! cried fate! to live and die an old maid. Isn't it shocking! I am sure I recommend myself to all and yet it does no good. If you can give me any advice, do, and you will favor me greatly.

But enough of this joking. I long very much to see you and my little nephew and nieces, nothing would gratify me so much as to come and see you. I can scarcely realize yet, the fact that you occupy the position of Wife and Mother. What a great change have six years wrought! You must tell me in your next what you are wearing and how the children look and if John wears "good clothes"? I think I remember his promising to write to me nearly a year ago and he has not yet done so. Ought I to forgive him? I will do so if he will not delay any longer. A young man belonging to our church is to set sail for England some time this month. This would be a first rate opportunity for one of us to visit you if everything else favored but I suppose we must exercise patience a little longer. We have not heard from my Aunt Lewis for a long time. Is John coming this Spring, I wish he would. Give my love to them and Bertha. And give ever so many kisses to the children from all of us. George often complains that you do not write to him. Excuse this badly written letter for I have written it just as it came out of my mind. Write very soon and do not forget

Your everloving Sister

Mary

Letter #20 – Mary to Emily

Troy Aug. 28th [1856]

My own Sister,

I as well as Mama, am ashamed that this letter has not been forwarded before, but if you will only forgive us this time you shall not have cause to complain again. You will see by the date of my other sheet, that Alfred would have time to write in my absence, but he tells me he will send a packet of his own just as soon as he can spare time. It is on his account these letters have been delayed so long.

I am glad to tell you that Mama is very much better now; this morning (7 o'clock) she is dressing to visit a lady who lives about 2 miles out of the city; she thinks the fresh air will do her good. I suppose she will return this afternoon. I have just received a scolding from her for leaving so much space at the top of the page, she says she will try to fill that herself.

George and I had "fine times" (as the Americans would say) down at Chatham. Our country cousins, during the few days we stayed with them, were very kind. We enjoyed ourselves extremely on riding out, one part of the country where we visited called Canaan has delightful scenery, after crossing a brook, Jordan, we reached a place which from the surrounding hills and rivulets reminded me strongly of ancient Jerusalem, close by was a mountain whose summit was practically hid in the clouds; it certainly was a soul stirring sight. We returned 2 days ago, more fully appreciating the warm hearts and pleasant society of country people.

Fred has had an offer to become Pianist to the "Euphomons" who are giving concerts all over the States. They will, on this tour, go south along the Mississippi to be gone six months. After some thought, Fred concluded not to go, he could not leave Ma. No doubt it would have done him good, but I do not know how we should have spared him. Well Emily, I feel as though I were getting old very fast, just think, I am approaching 21 years, and have no chance of getting married yet, when you were my age, you were all provided for, but poor me, will I am afraid always have to look out for myself. I use every means in my power to find someone who would be willing to take me "for better or for worse", but they prove utterly ineffectual.

I fear we have had a very strange summer, the weather has been exceedingly cool and windy, with the exception of about 3 weeks when the heat was almost intolerable and so dry, the gardens seemed burned up, flowers drooped and died, and even the trees were casting their leaves, the grass appeared yellow and dry, in the middle of July. After that we had 3 days of heavy rain, which produced such a change in the atmosphere that we needed fires and clothing. Such a cold season has caused everything in the shape of fruits and vegetables to be very dear, so we have not preserved much yet; we have done up a peck and a half of black currants, and I think about the same of plums. It is not time for quinces and peaches but I think that we shall not do many of those. Father is intending to write to John, but he has been very busy lately in making out catalogues to see if he can increase his business. We are afraid his bookstore will not answer. The trade has been very dull this summer and it is, likely, that it will be given up next spring. Alfred thinks he had better superintend a collar store again, as he expects at that time to enter into partnership himself with a young man who is already in that business, and from whom he has had an offer. If he can arrange the affair I think it will be very well for him. Alfred has not been very well, he has been troubled with indigestion for some weeks, but as he is going into the country for a week or so, we hope it will soon leave him. Fathers health is extremely good, he eats everything that is put before him in fact, his digestion and health are better than I have ever known it. Also Edmunds health is good, he grows very fast and will be stoutest of the family. Ma says he is just like my grandfather. My paper is full so my dear Emily Farewell:

[unsigned, from Mary]

Letter #21 – Brother Fred to Emily

Frederick is fifteen when he writes this amusing letter to his sister.

1857

My Dear Sister,

It is now mid-summer and here I am sitting in a rocking chair, writing to a dear sister in a distant land.

To day it is very warm, but we live in such a cool place among so many trees that we do not feel the heat till we go down into the city.

I cannot converse with you now, as I would were we standing face to face: but as I cannot enjoy that privilege, and have no hope of doing so, I must do as well as I can with my mind and pen.

How do the dear little children get along? Do they ever talk about their young uncles in America? Tell them their uncle Freddie sends his love to them. O but could I see your juvenile family. Could I but see their pleasing countenances, their bright eyes and smiles, it would be the greatest pleasure that I could imagine.

In the next garden next to ours is situated a house there, lives as it were my dear sister and her family, my reason for this is that it is equal to yours in size and numbers. It consists of a young lady and her husband, two very pretty and interesting children and a baby in arms.

In the next garden on the right on an eminence above the street, stands a beautiful house with four large handsome pillars in front, and a grapevine and fruit trees in the rear and the above described house will be vacated in a short time. Now I have given you a brief description of this house. Who do you think I would the future inmates to be? Can you guess? I think I hear you say "he wants us". That is it, but alas there is no HOPE!

On the ninth of July our Sunday school made an excursion to Hudson, a city situated on the west bank of the Hudson river about thirty five miles below Troy. The splendid steamer Comodore was hired for the occasion. We went to the school at seven Oclock and after singing a few hymns preparatory to the occasion, closed with prayer by the pastor and marched to the steamboat which started at ten o'clock. On our passage up and down the river the scenery was exceedingly beautiful. The woods, the green fields, the large towns and villages, the vessels and steamboats on the river and the immense rocks composed quite a romantic scene. On our arrival at Hudson which was about one o'clock, the school went into one of the churches of that city where we sang together and heard several interesting speeches by the minister. After remaining in Hudson about an hour, we returned to the steamboat. On our way home, nothing worthy of note occurred excepting when we were about half a mile above Albany, the steamer struck a sand bar and stuck fast. We remained in this predicament about two hours and a half enjoying ourselves very much when at eight o'clock a small steamer pulled us off. The time for us to have returned was 6 o'clock (for the steamer was to have gone to N. York at 7 1/2 o'clock) but on account of it getting aground, it did not land till three hours afterward. A young gentleman of our acquaintance fearing that Ma would be anxious, called his man with his carriage and informed her that we might be home about midnight.

We received brother John's photograph with much delight, but I did not recognize it at first he looks so much more manly. Give my love to him and tell him I wish very much to see him. Remember me to my dear Aunt Uncle and cousin John, and accept my very best love yourself my ever! dear!! dear!!! DEAR!!!! Emily

From your affectionate brother,

Frederick H. Cluett

~ ~ ~

Letter #22 – Ann to Emily

This letter from Ann to Emily is on the back of Frederick's letter in 1857.

My dear Emily,

As I am now better I will fill Freddy's letter up. Mary I think has not been explicit enough about my health. I will say a few words myself. Five weeks ago yesterday I was taken ill with a low viruous fever and my Doctor being in England (for he is an Englishman) I would not call in another, but thought I should get better as I had done before. However, when he returned which was three weeks after my attack, he was called in and said it was congestion of the liver with low fever. He gave me some medicine which acted upon me like magic. I believe if I had him at first I should not have kept my bed a week. However, I shall now know better for the future.

How are you all doing? I suppose in my mind's eye I see you in New St. fifty times in a day. I fancy John in his shop you sewing or nursing in your sitting room, and the children playing around you. I suppose the baby is now getting a fine girl. Kiss [her brow?] for her grandmama. Kiss them all for me. I should like to see them. Dear little creatures.

We are very much pleased with John's likeness we like it better than the other, but people say they soon fade. Alfred says he will have an Ambrotype [photograph] taken from that – and from your daguerreotype. He has put Johns in a beautiful case. I should have had your fathers and mine taken long ago, but they do now take them on paper. We are going to have them taken in Ambrotype, and you shall have them the first opportunity,

We received your uncle's welcome packet of letters last week, and found them very interesting indeed. I am sorry Bertha is going to marry a worldly minded man, which I fear he is. Tell us more about her when you write, give my love to her, and to Mrs. Grinsell. Tell her the children's portraits would be highly prized. We shall expect ----- of your children's with them.

Good bye my precious child, The Lord be with you and yours.

Amen

[Ann Cluett]

Letter #23 – William to Emily

When William writes Emily in the fall of 1858, it is eight years after emigrating and the family is now doing very well. William says, in addition to their music store in Troy, we have "*opened a fine store in Albany.*"

"*I scarcely know how our business has grown to its present magnitude. When I commenced four years ago I had but a small stock, but it has grown, by the blessing of Providence, to two large stores, well-filled.*"

"*I forget whether you have received any account of our present residence. I will write you a line or two about it anyway. It is located on one of the pleasantest streets in the City.*"

He goes on to tell her they have no more boarders, and "*plenty of room for the family and a spare bedroom for the casual visitor.*" They have a "*bookcase with double folding doors, well filled with (chiefly) good theological works, and a new Rosewood piano and a Reed organ with two stops and an octave of foot pedals*". "*We have parlors, bedrooms, and dining room all carpeted,*" and "*this is a great country for rocking chairs I think we have six.*" William's pleasure in being able to buy beautiful things is evident.

In this letter William also describes traveling to Philadelphia and looking up his cousins, meeting in person for the first time his father's sister, Elizabeth Newton. They are now financially comfortable enough to undertake such visits. After this, the two families travel regularly to spend time with each other. Mary Cluett later marries her peer in that family, her second cousin (Elizabeth's grandson), Reverend Joseph Newton Mulford.

By 1858, the family standing in the community has been achieved. With an appealing humorous self-mockery William begins his description of the family in Troy to Emily by saying, "*(I will just say here that in order to give you a correct idea of us, as a family, I may possibly write some lies which I would not have seen by other eyes than your own and John's,)*" and yet it is clear that he is pleased with the progress of his children and the regard with which the entire family is held:

"*… you would be much gratified if you could know the estimate of your sister and brothers by all who know them. Another such family is not to be found in the City of Troy. They are known as a Model Family. Your precious mother is often asked how she has made them what they are….*"

As to their trustworthiness in financial matters, "*By some means or other, I scarcely know, we have gained the public confidence to such a degree that our credit is good, both here and in New York* [City] *for almost any amount.*" William's remark "*I scarcely know how*", seems almost ironic but he appears sincere in his wonder.

Troy, N.Y. Oct 30, 1858

My very dear daughter Emily,

I have proposed writing you a long letter for many months, in fact, I did write the greater part of one, but became dissatisfied with it and threw it aside. You must not allow yourself to suppose you are forgotten, because the long letter I promised to send you has been so long in coming. You are not forgotten. I could not, if I would forget my precious first-born. And, there is a memento of you before me night and morning. The fox Head slippers are still doing good service, though somewhat dilapidated, and when they become no longer serviceable, I shall hang them up in quiet repose, for the sake of the donor. Though three thousand miles of water divides us, and though the separation has continued through more than eight long years, yet I have not relinquished the hope of again clasping my daughter to my bosom. I live in hope of yet finding myself in a position to visit England if Providence its mysterious operations should not bring you to the land of my adoption. Much as I have wished to see you all here with us, I have never strongly urged your coming on the principle that it is "best to let well alone".

Oh, how I wish you could visit us and see how we look! How we are situated and what we are doing. (I will just say here that in order to give you a correct idea of us, as a family, I may possibly write some lies which I would not have seen by other eyes than your own and John's.) I think you would be much gratified if you could know what is the estimate formed of your sister and brothers by all who know them. Another such family is not to be found in the City of Troy. They are known as a Model Family. Your precious mother is often asked how she has made them what they are. To give you an idea of the estimate formed of their integrity, I may mention that the proprietor of one of the Lace stores in the city always sends for Robert to remain with his hands in the store during his absence in New York. By some means or other, I scarcely know how, we have gained the public confidence to such a degree that our credit is good, both here and in New York for almost any amount.

Mary has won for herself the esteem and admiration of everyone acquainted with her. Her perseverance in business is indefatigable. She has many more pupils than any other female teacher has, or ever has in the place. At a Sacred concert given in one of the churches a week or two since, she sang the beautiful solo, "With Verdure Clad" in a masterly style. Several Professors present pronounced it the best executed during the concert, although the best talent in the city was employed. I think you would be gratified to listen to Freddy's performance on one of Chickering's Grand Pianos. He bids fair to become one of the best pianists in the country. He possesses, not only perseverance, but also skill and taste and with these qualifications I know nothing that can prevent his climbing to the top of the trees.

I forgot whether you were informed by Mary when she wrote last, that we had opened a fine store in Albany. We commenced operations there last May. The store has plate glass windows and is

(I think) from seventy to eighty feet in length. The principal part of the business is that of Sheet music and musical instruments, though we, also, keep stock of books. So far, the business has been very encouraging, though it has been the dullest portion of the year. Alfred and Freddy attend to this store and I visit them once a week, and sometimes oftener. One of them generally comes up to Troy on Saturday night and remains till Monday morning. They give the result of the undertaking. I scarcely know how our business has grown to its present magnitude. When I commenced four years ago I had but a small stock, but it has grown, by the blessing of Providence to two large stores, well-filled. Our business in Troy is better this season than ever before. In fact, it is too large for the store and we are calculating upon getting possession of the adjoining store, which is larger than the present one, and has besides the advantage of double frontage. We often wish John was with us to help it along. We want a store in New York City; it would be a great advantage to us.

George is still in the Collar business, but will leave it and come into one of the stores next Spring, if the prospects should be sufficiently considered encouraging to authorize that stop. He has a fine voice and is thought by many to be the best Tenor singer in the place. Robert is practicing two or three hours a day on the piano, and will make a good player. He has business tact, too, fully equal, if not superior to the rest of the boys. Edmund had to leave his hardware business to come into the Troy store with us. He plays pretty well on the violin, but has not perseverance enough to practice sufficiently to excel.

I forget whether you have received any account of our present residence. I will write you a line or two about it anyway. It is located on one of the pleasantest streets in the City. It reminds us of the Castle Hill in Bridgnorth. We (that is, your mama and I) often talk of the Castle Hill, during our walks on Eight Street. We have a fine view of the Hudson River, north and south – the City of Albany, the villages of Lansingburg, Waterford, and Cohoes, besides overlooking the City of Troy in its entire length. We have, also, a fine view of the Catskill Mts. and a wide extent of country. Much of this is also seen from our back windows. The house itself suits us well. We have plenty of room for the family and a spare bedroom for the casual visitor. We cannot boast of any expensive furniture, as money is too valuable to be locked in that article. The three most important articles consist of a bookcase, with double folding doors, well filled with (chiefly) good Theological works, and a new Rosewood piano and a Reed organ with two stops and an octave of foot-pedals. I think I have told you that this is a great country for carpets and we have Parlors, bedrooms, dining-room, all carpeted, except the cooking kitchen. I was near forgetting to tell you that this is a great country for Rocking Chairs, I think we have six.

I believe Mary told you in her last letter that we found some relatives. I went to New York about two months since, to purchase books, etc., but not finding what I wanted, I concluded to go at once to Philadelphia. I had felt anxious to visit that city ever since we came here, because I know my Uncle, Aunt and Cousins emigrated there when I was a little boy, but business did not see to call me there and I hesitated about incurring the expense of the journey. I now resolved to find out, if possible, if any or all of them were still living. I did not arrive there till after eight o'clock in the evening, but after I had taken my supper at the hotel, I went to the clerk in the office and inquired if he had a directory. He handed one to me and I found ten or fifteen of the name "Newton". In looking down the list I saw one "Newton", Rev. Richard, and as that was my uncle's name, I copied the address first on my list, proposing to make my first call upon him.

I rose in the morning about half-past five and set off to look at the City. (and a fine City it is) I walked until between seven and eight o'clock, when I set off to find "Rev. R. Newton", and I supposed somebody would be stirring at that time. I found the house with the name on the door and rang the bell. Presently, a steady looking servant came to the door and I asked if "Rev. Mr. Newton was within?" She answered that both Mr. and Mrs. Newton were in the country and were not expected home before the following week. At this I felt disappointed and was about leaving when she asked if I could leave my message. I replied, I had not any message to leave, but wished to ask Mr. Newton if he or his parents came from England. She answered, "yes, they did come from England and if you will step into the parlour, I will call Mrs. Newton down." I said, "I understood you to say that Mrs. Newton was from home." "Yes, she said, but I mean old Mrs. Newton; Mr. Newton's Mother." I now began to be considerably excited and walked into the parlor. After I had sat for a few minutes an old lady walked into the room and I felt somewhat embarrassed to know how to proceed. I told her I was inquiring after some relatives as I was informed she came from England, I should be glad to know from what part of England she came. She answered "From Burcott in Shropshire". I asked, "What was your father's name?" John Cluett, she replied. I now felt certain of being on the right track and asked her if she had any brother and what was his name? She said she had one brother and his name was William. "And I am the son of that brother William", I answered.

You must imagine the astonishment of both parties, for I cannot describe it. The discovery seemed to each of us too marvelous to be true and we could scarcely credit the reality. It seemed too much like a dream. It was, however, no "baseless fabric of a vision", for there stood my father's aged sister, erect, though bearing the burden of eighty winters, and there was I, her only brother's only son. The only regret was on account of the absence of my cousin and his wife. Of course I had many explanations to give and to receive. My uncle died before we came into the country. The Rev. R. Newton is Minister of St. Paul's Episcopal Church in Philadelphia and a Doctor of Divinity. Another of my cousins is an Episcopal Minister, another a Methodist Minister. I was obliged to leave for home on the evening of the day on which I made the discovery business calling me away.

On my return I greatly astonished your mama and the rest of the family by the budget of news I had to open. We shortly afterwards sent my Aunt, the Doctor and his wife a pressing invitation to visit us in Troy and about a month since my Aunt and the Doctor came, but Mrs. Newton, Jr. could not leave home. I cannot tell you what an event their visit was in the family. I can only ask you to imagine what you would have felt in like circumstances if you had not seen a solitary individual for more than eight years, whom you could claim as a relative in the most remote degree. We found the Doctor to be a most devoted and laborious Minister of Jesus Christ and one of the most spiritual men we have ever met. My aunt, though over eighty years of age, bore the long journey well. As far as we could judge, their gratification was as great as our own at the union of the two families after so long a separation. They had not seen a blood relative for more than thirty years. As the Doctor's engagements rendered it impossible for him to remain longer, they only passed three days with us, but if all be well, they will, also visit us again next summer. I expect business to call me to New York next week (this October 30) in which case Mary will go with me and we shall visit Philadelphia together, remaining over Sunday. I can assure you this discovery and visit has been to us All the most interesting event that has occurred the last eight years. The Christmas and New Year's Day have come around and our neighbors and friends have been visited by their brothers and sisters and cousins, etc. and one or another in the family has said, "Oh, how pleasant it would be if we had some relatives who could visit us." This desire (In God's providence) has at last been gratified.

And now we have only one wish in that direction at least, ungratified, and that is to see some of our much-loved and far-distant friends in England. When this wish will be gratified we know not, seeing it lies in the dark, mysterious future. I would like for you to acquaint Sister Radnale, when you see her, with the above particulars relating to my Aunt and family. I have not yet made any reference to your mama in this letter. I am happy to report that her health is quite as good, perhaps better, than it has been for some time. We ramble over the fields and hills and woods together when the weather is fine, and enjoy ourselves as much as we did in our youthful days. Our honeymoon has not waned yet, though we have encountered together many of the storms and disappointments and ills incident to human life. She was never more precious to me, not even in the hour when she pledged her faith to me at the altar; than she is at present. I suppose our wedded life has been so far, as happy and harmonious as ever falls to the lot of mortals and I do not think that anything is likely to occur to mar that harmony. If her health was as robust as once it was I suppose our happiness would be too great.

Nov. 3. Mary and I leave by the Steamboat for New York this evening, thence by rail to Philadelphia in the morning. I wanted to write a great deal more, but my paper is nearly filled and I am doubtful about getting what I have written into a single postage. If I can put it in, you will find enclosed a small engraving which will give you a little idea of our city. Give my best love to John and also to your Aunt and Uncle Lewis and kiss the children for me. How every much I would like to see them. Your mama and all the children unite in love to you all. She intended to have written a few lines in this letter, but I have no room to spare so you must excuse her this time.

Before I close let me say to you, as I have said before, "If trade should fail and prospects prove dark, don't hesitate to cross the Atlantic". The children will do better here.

I am, my very dear Emily,
Your affectionate father,

W.C. [William Cluett]

William's goal of restoring the appearance of his family's integrity has been accomplished. To do this he has needed to keep the circumstances of their flight to America secret, which he does with Ann's cooperation and support.

Letter #24 – William to Emily

Four years have passed since the last letter. It is clear that the Cluett family has been doing well; however, as affected so many others, the Cluett family lost their house in the Great Fire of Troy in 1862. William writes to Emily about the loss of their house, and to tell her that a new house has been purchased. William notes that it is located "*on one of our aristocratic streets.*"

"*(I will tell you) ... particulars of the fire.... I found the nice house I had left so recently a heap of ruins. I had 300 or 400 dollars in the drawer in my bedroom most of it in gold and silver...*" which he loses. William managed to dig out about $220 in gold and silver after the fire.

"*... We had lost house, furniture, apparel, everything,*" but they were "*tolerably well insured.*"

At this point, twelve years after migration, William has money to complete the repayment of his creditors, but apparently does not.

"*We have purchased a new residence and removed to it, when I tell you the price of it you will begin to think that the great fire has not done us any great harm. The price of the house and premises is $7,000 or nearly 1,500 pounds. We do not have to pay the whole of the purchase money down, or we would not have had the place. Our credit happens to be so good, that we can purchase at any time you choose.*"

William seems amazed that their credit is as good as it is, and he uses it to buy a fine house.

"*Your mama is much pleased with it... we looked at many... but (she found them) objectionable... and had to give them up.*" Ann's ambitions support their continued movement up materially and socially.

William goes on, "*...we have been so extravagant as to furnish our bedrooms uniformly from top to bottom (one room chestnut, one room black walnut, one room mahogany, and so forth.)*" The parlor "*took over 70 yards to carpet.... you will wonder how we can do all this.... Union is strength.*" Again, William and Ann link prosperity with moral worth.

Troy July 8, 1862

My Dear Daughter Emily,

I have been intending to commence a letter for 3 or 4 weeks, & when your most welcome letter was received, I thought I would reply immediately; but we have been so full of business that it has not deemed possible. In fact, we have so much to do, that I have not had time for my favorite amusement, fishing. Our business this year is much greater than it ever was before, so you see the war [the American Civil War] is not ruining us. We have the finest assortment of Piano Fortes in the State of New York, & the sale of them has been very good. In one week we sold five, at prices varying from 250 to 300 Dollars each. Alfred sold one this morning before dinner.

I did not see the letter your Mamma sent, but I [suppose] she gave you some particulars of the fire. O what a terrible desolation in the short space of about 3 hours! I left the dinner table about ½ past 12 oclock & the fire spread with such fearful rapidity, that I was cut off from all approaches to Eighth St. till about 4 oclock, & then I found the nice house I had so recently left, a heap of ruins. I had 300 or 400 Dollars in the drawer in my bedroom most of it in gold and silver, & the boys broke the lock & carried the drawer and its contents to the beautiful mansion of a neighbor opposite, supposing it would be perfectly safe there. But that home was burnt too, & the money with it. We thought it was all lost, but a week or two afterwards, we were so fortunate as to dig out of the ruins about 220 Dollars in gold & Silver. We were tolerably well insured, or our loss would have been very great. As it is, we may safely set it down at 1500 Dollars, at least, or £300 sterling. This, you seem to think, is a terrible loss, & it is a really large sum to lose, & it was a great deal of labor to get together; but we were so thankful that the whole family had escaped uninjured, & that our business was spared to us, that we have given ourselves little concern about what we have lost. If you could have seen us on the evening of the fire, when gathered in the cottage that was providentially open for us, you would not have supposed from our merriment, that we had lost House, Furniture, apparel, & almost everything. The children said, "Never mind it, Father, we are all young, healthy, & industrious. We will put our shoulders to the wheel, & soon recover all we have lost." Although so many hundreds were placed in precisely the same circumstances as ourselves, yet we found numerous Kind friends, who urged us to accept their hospitalities. We were, in fact, overloaded with Kindness.

We have purchased a new residence, & removed to it; & when I tell you what was the price of it, you will begin to think that the great fire has not done us any great harm. The price of the House & premises is 7000 Dollars, or nearly £1500. We do not have to pay the whole of the purchase money down, or we would not have had the place. Our credit happens to be so good, that we can purchase at any time we choose. The House is a very nice one, & the whole family is delighted with it. It is located on one of our aristocratic streets, & comprises 2 lots, each 25 feet wide, by 130 feet deep. We have now got what I have long wanted, - a nice garden. The prospects are very promising for a nice crop of Grapes, Peaches, & Plums. One thing in relation to the place delights me very much, & that is, your Mamma is much pleased with it. We have looked over a number of nice houses, but the location, or some interior arrangement, was objectionable to her, & we had to give them up, one after another. We have now room to accommodate you & all the family, when you arrive.

The furnishing of it has cost considerable, as we lost nearly all we had by the fire. Many persons, both in this, & other cities, who occupy nice houses, are particularly careful to have their parlours elegantly furnished, & leave their bedrooms half empty. But we have gone ----- upon a different principle. We have been so extravagant as to furnish our rooms uniformly from top to bottom. Alfred's bedroom has a suite of Chesnut Furniture, with marble top to Bureau tc [etc]. George's is Black Walnut, finished in oil, - a beautiful set. Mary's is mahogany. Edmund's is Black Walnut, & Fred's & Robert's painted in imitation of Chesnut. Nearly all the bedrooms have stationary marble top wash stands, with hot and cold water taps. We have a nice Wash Room & water closet. The rooms are all supplied with gas from the basement to the third story, & in such good condition that we have not laid out a dollar in paint or ----- . The parlour is what is known here, as a "Saloon Parlour", that is, one large room, not divided by folding doors. It took over 70 yds, of Carpet to cover it. It is beautiful velvet carpet & cost us about £25. The Pier [?] glass between the front windows, rests on a marble slab, is about 9 feet in length, & cost £ 25. The room is ornamented with a costly ----- of moulding and fret work. There is a beautiful chandelier in the centre, consisting of 6 Burners. Our Piano is a large 7¼ octave in carved rosewood case, 4 round corners, finished all round, & carved legs. I met ----- with it in New York the other day at a bargain. I find I cannot give a catalogue & price of the Spanish Mahogany Chairs, Sofas, Marble top Tables, tc. [etc] as my sheet is almost full. The sitting room, Dining Room, & small kitchen, are all in range behind the Parlour. The large cooking kitchen is in the Basement. We also have an excellent 2 storey stable & Carriage house, & according to the talk of the boys, the next extravagance will be a Horse & Carriage. You will perhaps wonder how we can do all this, but the explanation is very easily given. Union is strength. As a family we have held firmly together, considering that the interest of one is the interest of all; & so long as we continue to hold together, we shall very easily ac ------------

[No more of this letter exists. Although no signature appears, it is clearly from Emily's father, William Cluett.]

Letter #25 – Ann to Emily

Ann writes Emily in 1862 as the Civil War continues. Business now prospers but "oh! what a state (the country) is now in... the dreadful war," meaning the American Civil War, 1861-1865. However, George, now in the collar industry, "*has been making money fast*."

While devastation, both physical and financial, was widespread in the South, there was a great deal of prosperity in the North over the years of the American Civil War, with the expansion of industry and the demand for goods.

As for servants, Ann says, "*I have two.*" After their early financial struggles, the Cluetts are now well situated, living on one of the 'aristocratic streets', and with two servants to help Ann in the running of the house.

Ann also refers to aunts and an uncle in England: her sister and brother, Aunt Lewis (who later moves from England to live with the Cluetts) and Uncle Bywater, and William's sister Aunt Radnale. John Lewis (son of Aunt Lewis) is one of three Johns in the letters, referred to by the Cluetts as Big John (John Cadby Sr.), Middle John (John Lewis) and Small John (John Cadby Jr.)

Troy August 13, 1862

My dear Emily,

[The first part of this letter is too faded to read.]

...She [Polly, Emily's daughter who is visiting the Cluetts in Troy] is anxious to be a good pianist and says she will not want to come home for 2 or 3 years yet. She says she would like to come for one thing, and that is to see her grandmother. She would like to see you all but her grandmother being old she thinks she may not live till that time, and she rather hopes she will not for fear she might become childish like Mrs. Newton of Philadelphia.

I am sorry to tell you that she lost all her keepsakes at the fire. She had them in a little box inside her drawer in her bedroom, and no one could get to her room after the fire commenced. She asked me previous to that to let her take your portrait that John sent her, and put among her other things, and I am sorry to say that was burnt. All the other portraits, and most of the presents that Edmund brought with him were saved, being suitable for parlour tables, or to carry in the pockets. The knife your Uncle Lewis sent for Alfred, he had given to me for safe keeping, and it was put up in a box and was lost together with Mary's fan, my neck tie and collar. I believe everything else was saved. After the fire commenced, Mary told one of the girls to bring her a large clothes basket so she snatched the things off the parlour tables and put them into it, and left it with the furniture. Robert's table was saved.

I suppose you would like to know how the boys matrimonial affairs are progressing. Alfred has selected his wife at last, and a greater contrast in a couple you never saw. He is literary, a great thinker, and a great reader (indeed so much so that he makes friends with most of the college students) and she is an airy light fancy girl of twenty summers. She is rather handsome and a good figure. I think she has good sense, but she lost her mother when she was very young, and has not had a proper training. Her father keeps a boot & shoe store in the city, and is a member of our church, so is she. Her name is Lilly ~~Bonacue~~ Lillie Bontecue. She is cousin to Sarah Golden, George's girl, Edmund and his girl have parted, I believe, he said something that she did not like, so she put on airs, and he left her. His health is rather better lately, and his business is good. He was disappointed in not receiving a letter from you. I think he was very much vexed.

We have had Robert very ill with Diptheria, a dangerous complaint. We had prompt aid, and he was better in a few days, but he has not yet recovered his strength, and it has left him with very weak eyes. He is able however to attend to his business. He is at George's store now and will do well. That is, if the country prospers, but oh! What a state it is now in. We know not what is coming, nor what will be the result of this dreadful war. They talk of pressing men soon, as they do not offer themselves fast enough. I tremble for the consequences.

I am sorry to hear that you are so much troubled with rheumatism. I cannot see why it is. I hope by this time the warm weather has helped you, with the assistance of the [quiacam ?]. It is a painful complaint and it makes me feel anxious about you.

Polly and I often talk about you all. When she sees any little girl she says that is the size of Annie or that is the size of Emmy. I would give the world, if I possessed it, to see them all. You must tell us a good deal about them in your letter. I wish they could have seen their uncles, Polly, and myself this morning in the grape arbour where we were sitting enjoying its cooling shade from a burning sun. How they tossed Polly about, and how delighted she was. One would tickle her with grass another would take her chair from under her and so on. She likes nothing better than a bit of fun with her uncles. I know you all want to see her very much but you must not be anxious about her for she is well, and well cared for.

My own health is some better, perhaps it is in answer to prayer. What an unspeakable blessing it is to have praying children. How good is the Lord. May He in His mercy grant that my children and my children's children may all be numbered among His jewels when He shall count them up. My constant prayer is that not a cast-away may be found among my descendents to the latest generation.

Your account of your Aunt Lewis is discouraging and very bad. The doctor may be mistaken. She has a strong constitution. I am not without hope that I shall see her again before I leave the shores of time. Tell her to write me. She owes me a letter. Poor John Lewis, I am sorry for him to be tied down to a woman so much older than himself, and a Unitarian, too. We all think he ought not to be bound to have her as he was under age when he promised her, and being young and thoughtless is scarcely to be considered ----- . I fear if he ----- it will be the ruin of him. I should advise him to come over here if it were not for the war. But it will not do now.

[The next lines are too faded to read.]

Mary has gone into the country to stay a week. Her health has been down from too much ----- .

I hope to see you all here when this country is once more restored to peace. A man as ----- as John could not fail to do well here. Besides, his children would do better. John could be educated at ----- , and if he wished to be an Episcopal minister Doctor Newton would put him in the way, and when he was ready, find him a ----- . He would have done so ----- any of our boys if they had been inclined.

Tell us in your next how your Aunt Radnale is doing. I would like to know how your Uncle Bywater is. I thought of writing to him before this, but have been so busy. Polly and I have been in the field this afternoon catching grasshoppers for bait, and Alfred and Robert have gone fishing and I expect they will bring home a nice lot for breakfast. George has gone to take his lady out riding.

Polly's likeness together with George and Alfred's girls will come next time. George liked his suit of clothes very much. I believe they were your choice. He has been making money fast.

I have been sadly -------------- with a girl, but now I hope I have two that suit me. It is very hot weather now and I feel very languid. In a little while it will be more moderate and then I hope to be better.

You affectionate mother,

Ann Cluett

Letter #26 – William to John

William remarks on the dramatic change in their circumstances, from the threat of ruin in England, to financial security. He says that while he was worried for the future of his children in England, now no more. *"I have no anxiety now... I consider this a great blessing purchased at a comparatively trifling cost ..."*

The *"comparatively trifling cost"* is presumably that of having left all that he valued in England, including his good reputation, in order to flee his overwhelming financial obligations.

Troy Sep 19, 1863

My Dear Son John,

Emily's letter rec'd yesterday, brings us the agreeable intelligence that you are turning your thoughts towards the New World. I have been for some time expecting to hear of this & I may say that I rejoice to hear it, not only for the reason that we shall be brought nearer together, but because we have long felt, that with your large family, & well known habit of industry & perseverance, you ought to be here. Even if your own circumstances should not be greatly improved by the change, you will be more than satisfied by the prospects it will open to the children. If thousands in England only knew the advantages this country presents to an industrious man with a large family, the numbers of immigrants, large as they are now reported every week, would be astonishingly increased. We have for several years thought that you could be advantageously located in New York City. It is a wonderful place for trade, & great bargains are constantly turning up. The second-hand trade in Troy, (with the exception of School Books), is a poor affair, but in New York large quantities are sold, in consequence of the great influx of merchants & visitors from all parts of the Union. Some of the Booksellers told me, the last time I was down there, that with my knowledge of the business, & the strength of the Firm, we ought to be in N. Y. I have no doubt we could make money faster, but we should have to submit to a great sacrifice to go there. I am acquainted with a Bookseller who keeps a very large stock of English Books of all classes, & who is going down to his grave very fast. I have thought, that in the event of his death, it would be a first-rate opening for you, if it were possible to purchase the stock at a reasonable price. At any rate, I am sufficiently well acquainted with the streets to determine which are the best business locations. We should all prefer to see you permanently located in Troy, if such an arrangement could be made. We have talked over several suggestions in relation to this. George thinks if Mr. Maullin could be brought to sell out his interest in the business, there would be a first rate opening for you there. This would be first rate, as the collar business is much better than ours. We often think we made a great mistake in not commencing in that line, instead of our present one. Then I have had some conversation with the boys as to whether it would be possible, as to enlarge our business, with what stock & capital you could command as to warrant the taking you into our concern. I should like this myself, but before your coming we shall have time & opportunity to canvas these, & any other propositions or thoughts that may be suggested. Your knowledge of the Book trade at home would not be of much value to you here, for the reason that your new Books differ so greatly from ours in price. My impression is, that new books published in England at 21/, would not be priced here at more than one half that sum. As regards bringing your stock, or a part of it with you, I wish I could be there to make the selection. I would do it much better than I can give the necessary directions. Don't bring any common School Books, nor any of the Poets, unless they are the best editions in good preservation. I have found that the buyers of old books are more particular about the condition of them here, than they are with you. I think you would be safe in bringing any good editions of the Greek & Latin -------------- , good copies of Clarke's, Berwin's, H ----- , Scotts', G ----- & other commentaries on the -------------- The works of the leading English ----- such as Owen, ---------- , Barrow, ---------- etc. etc; – good bound copies of Rollin, Gibbon, Hume, & ---------- & other standard Historians; – the old ---------- Theology of 1600 to 1700; – ---------- Encyclopedias in good condition; old Books on America, & illustrated works. These, I think, would be safe properly to bring with you, that is, unless you can sell them for a good fair price at home. If you can, I think it would be better to bring the cash. If you should decide upon coming, you would do well to keep that thought constantly before you; — to make all your sales & purchases with reference to that design. I would not buy any Books that I did not consider likely to sell quickly, or to be well worth bringing her.

You will bear in mind that it is not absolutely necessary that you should embark in the book trade. There are many other ways of making money besides selling Books. It seems to be the rule here, for persons to change their business till they hit upon a profitable one. One of the wealthiest Collar Makers in this city was a Carpenter, & another was a Mason. If a Blacksmith thinks his business does not pay well enough, he will sell out, & open a clothing Store. There will be time & opportunity for future correspondence on this matter. As soon as it is possible for you to fix the probable time of your coming, let us know immediately, that we may be on the lookout for some opening. Of course it would not be a very dreadful thing, if you were not to engage in any business for a month or two. It would give you the opportunity of acquainting yourself of our modes of doing business, the currency, tc. Very likely, in contemplating this change, a great number of queries will rise in your mind, which you would like to have answered. If so, commit them to paper in your next letter, & we will answer them as fully as we can.

Our business is very good. There are four of us, & yet we find our hands full. We have recently leased the store adjoining ours, & in the Spring the two stores will be made one. Our front will have 3 plate glass windows, & 2 doors, & will surpass everything on the street. Our rent will be 1200 Dollars, or over 240 per annum. You will think this is a pretty steep rent, but we expect our business to increase in larger proportion than the rent.

We often hear it said, "This is a great country", & it is a true saying. Only think for a moment, – the State of New York is larger than the whole of England, & there are more than 30 States, several of them larger than New York! We have been engaged in an expensive war for more than two years, & yet the northern States do not appear to have felt the burden. Everything indicates great prosperity. We are, of course, paying additional taxes, but the country could never better afford to pay them. The war can only end in the triumph of the Federal ------------------------ unnatural & infamous attempt to divide the Union, & the destruction of that ---------------

--------- source of all our troubles, Slavery. This accomplished, the Slave States will be open to Northern men & Northern capital, & who shall prescribe limits to the tide of prosperity that will roll through this vast Union?

It is no small thing for a man to be relieved of anxiety in relation to the future of his family. Before I left England, this had become a great burden to me, for the future was all dark. But years ago, this burden was lifted off my heart, & the darkness turned to day. I have no anxiety now. If in the good providence of God, I should be called to leave them tomorrow, I should feel perfectly sure of His well doing. I consider this a great blessing purchased at a comparatively trifling cost. In England, a large family, to a poor man, is a heavy load of expense; here a source of wealth & prosperity.

We have been so busy, I have written this letter "a little bit at a time", you will, therefore, be likely to find it somewhat unconnected; but if you fail to understand any part of it, let me know, & I will send you a commentary. Write to me as soon as you can find time, & don't hesitate to ask questions on all subjects you feel to be of interest to you.

Your affectionate father,

W.C.

Letter #27 – Mary to Emily

This letter from Mary to Emily evidently follows a visit to Emily by Mary and her new husband Rev. Joseph Mulford. A rift has occurred, between John Cadby, and the Mulfords, perhaps relating to some urging on the part of Mary and Joseph that John should "*become a Christian.*" The rift is referred to briefly in later letters.

[July] 1864

My Dear Emily

I had waited anxiously for a message from you and was quite ready to devour its contents on its arrival; it seemed so like you for your letters are like Ma's every word tells and is intended for some purpose it contained much information about your family which you I am always pleased to hear. I should write to Polly this time but Joseph has just told me how much paper he will use so tell my little name-sake that I will make room for her next time, and then I will try to send a few words to the others in rotation. I never want those scenes of pushing to be repeated! Some one said to me yesterday that it would be very pleasant for Joseph and myself to visit you in a year or two, but oh, that time of goodbyes must not be endured a third time; I do not think that I could ever part with you and precious again.

I am surprised at what you say of John Lewis. Why ever does he wish to come to Canada? I suppose my Aunt will be with us shortly; poor woman, she has had sad trials in her life and gladly will we welcome her to our home and hope that her last days will be her best days. It is a pity that Harriet has left just at this time you must have altogether too much on your hands, perhaps I should be bewildered; well we are each in the spere [sphere ?] that is best suited to us for I know you would not like seeing so much company as I, you would find it a great bore, but to me it is not at all unpleasant except when I know people come to the rectory out of curiousity to see the "parson's wife". Four weeks today I came to my new home, and indeed Emily I can tell you that these four weeks have passed far more pleasurably than I could have imagined; you know I have said that I thought that for many reasons the first few weeks of married life must be the hardest, but if all are like these four we shall never have an unkind look or word.

It is now after four; I am writing in the study at Joseph's desk while he is out visiting; he will come home wet for the thunder is rolling heavily along the heaven. Our house is quiet – but not unpleasantly so, its inmates are Joseph, his mother, myself and the servant. We rise at half after five, after dressing Joseph likes a short walk and then stays in his study till seven when the breakfast bell rings, collecting first for prayers, after breakfast I am busy about the house and he goes to his studies till eleven; from that time till one he either ----- or reads with me and in the afternoon he visits his parishioners. You see I have abundance of time for reading and sewing and I am allowed to sit in the study as much as I like providing I do not interrupt his writing. The more I mix with the people the more I am pleased with them. They make me feel quite at home. We take tea at six; on Friday night we have prayermeeting and retire about ten. Sat. near five.

Have just read your letters; oh Emily my heart bleeds at the perusal of your note! I am just going with Joseph to Dr. Newton's to tea and consequently must put on a pleasant exterior but oh!

Mon. I am again alone Joseph has gone out; it is a pleasure to write to you for oh! I feel our separation so keenly. I am with you constantly in thought although I have everything about me so delightful I cannot if I wished it help a stray thought finding a resting place in New St.

I'm glad Aunt is coming only that you will be left entirely alone but it will certainly be the best for her to do as she needs to be with Ma. You were in a sorry mood when you wrote your last; but I cannot wonder when I think of your condition but you must cheer up and not allow anything to trouble you or your health will be undermined and that you know will never do for your family. I am grieved that 'precious' is unwell and that brow you have all but worshipped is wrinkled with care isn't it hard for you to bear?

You will be surprised that I send a letter to John, but as Joseph knew I had begun a letter to him, I thought it would appear strange to alter my purpose. You need not shew it to him however. Emily you know something of what my grief is to hear about our poor dear John. Why should he be so changeful in his efforts to do right? Why did I cross the Atlantic to cause you so much suffering? Did I do wrong when I was with you? Oh it almost distracts me to think of your sorrow and yet as you do I have to keep all this anxiety to myself. Cant you prevail on him to hear from me and become accustomed to my change of life. What, am I ever to have another letter from him? What will Joseph say? Do encourage him to seek to be a christian! It is awful to think he has made up his mind to give up trying. What will be done? For your sake my dear Sister he ought to be bright and cheerful you have enough of real sorrow. No one has seen your note but you must write a little only in the letter proper (not a separate sheet of paper) and place it in brackets so that when I am reading loud to Joseph I may know what to omit. I shall simply say "there is a part I do not wish to read". At dinner today I remarked

"I am going to write to Emily a little sheet for John not to see". Joseph at once said he did not think that was right for John would not like to know that anything should pass between us about which he knew nothing, well of course I saw where I stood and that he would not like me to have any letters he could not read. After dinner I asked if he still maintained that opinion? I found he did. He put on his hat and kissed me goodbye as he was going out for a while and when he was gone how could I help crying a little? When he came back he spoke very tenderly and told me to do as I thought best. I want to hear from you very very very soon for I shall be anxious about John. Oh do not let him remain in so much discouragement – he must be roused. What can we do but pray? I never knew such a care before. I cannot be happy while I know you are suffering so much. The more I am with Joseph the more I think you were mistaken in your opinion about him. My views are not changed and he suits me in that ------------------- in fact I did not know any man was like him and he is only too pleased to find my views so well agree with his own. Isn't it singular that I should meet with such a husband? I do enjoy praying with him and always feel glad when he closes the study door and says "Mary shall we have a word of prayer?" He is very kind to me and thoughtful of my happiness. Oh Emily I do not deserve such blessings I am highly favor'd. As a secret I will tell you that a vacancy has occurred in Troy and one of the vestrymen spoke to father about giving Joseph a "call"! What if we should remove to Troy? Wouldn't it seem strange? You need not refer to this in your next letter as nothing may grow out of it but it is singular that this church the only one in Troy I would choose for Joseph and the one in which Edmund plays should be vacant, and that Joseph's name should be mentioned as the new rector. I Well I hope we shall be led rightly. I am satisfied to remain here if it be best. I will write again soon; in the meantime let me know all about dear "precious". I will not write to him again till I have heard from you My dear darling Sister. I ------------------- you and yours constantly to God. May he be your support in this dark dark hour.

Your sympathizing

Mary

Letter #28 – Ann to Emily

[undated]
[8th child born 6 Sept. 1864]

My dear child

I am very, very thankful to learn that you are safely over your eighth trouble, and now I hope you are fast recovering, if you have not already become strong and healthy. I think a great deal about you, and all the family. I do sincerely hope and pray that you may be strong in body and mind to fill your responsible ------ in training your precious charge in the nurture and admonition of the Lord. John, I know will help you in all his power, and right thankful you ought to be that you have a partner so willing, and so well calculated to share in your anxieties and pleasures. (I have heard all about him, and tell him I love him as an own son,) You know you enjoy priviledge and pleasures I have always been a stranger to. I think a woman can be happy under almost any circumstances if her husband will take an interest in her affairs, as well as his own.

Your aunt, as you already know, has arrived safe and sound. She is in much better health that I expected to find her and seems very happy. I am extremely glad she has come. The boys are all fond of her, and are anxious to do all they can to make her feel at home. She appears to admire everything she sees. Freddy told her the other day that he believed if he told her "Old Nick" was beautiful, She would exclaim, "O yes, very beautiful."

I am glad to hear that you are going to remain into the country. I think it is a very good idea, if you can be satisfied away from John all day. You will be better in health, the children will be better, and enjoy themselves much more. I shall be very much pleased to hear that you have a nice country cottage, with plenty of poultry, and a good daily ----- such a one as Mary would make. I think it would be splendid.

I am sorry you did not receive my last letter, it was full of nice little silly things. Rejoice with me that Mary has come back to live at Troy, and Oh, that you could come, too, but I have no doubt that time will come. Give my love to John. Tell him I want to see him as badly as I want to see you and the children.

With much love I remain your affect'ant
Mother

Ann Cluett

Letter #29 – Ann To Emily

In this letter from Ann to Emily in 1864 — now fourteen years after their migration — the children are independent and the family is prosperous.

Ann says to Emily, *"Your father and I have been talking lately about his debts in England and have concluded, as soon as gold is at par, to pay them without the interest. Will you send Mr. Ward the account and he shall be paid if no one else is, but I have saved nearly enough to pay everyone myself, out of my housekeeping money, which I have out at interest, nearly 300 pounds (or $1,400), and that as far as I know would pay everyone off, but your father will do it himself, when gold is down."*

Although Ann still feels the obligation of the debts, she has no intention of repaying the debts when gold is high, and not ever with interest (although she is earning interest herself on her "*housekeeping money*"). Her belief in the moral justifiability of their original defection appears unchanged, and in her eyes apparently sanctioned by God, to the degree that she feels no particular compunction about a speedy (or financially fair) recompense.

Ann adds, about her grandchildren in England, *"Train them up in the fear of the Lord."*

[undated]

My dear child,

I am very thankful to learn that you are safely over your eighth difficulty, and have good health, and spirits to perform your marriage duties. I hope, by this time the baby is better, for there is nothing more trying to parents than seeing the suffering of an innocent baby. You must have your hands very full. I wish you could be relieved of the duties of the store, for your household cares are heavy enough for the strongest constitution. How is John? I hope his health is good, for it is all important. Give my love to him, and tell him one kiss from him would be worth a thousand pounds. Your aunt and I often talk about you all. The other day I made up some verses for your amusement. It is not worth reading, but I thought I would send it. When you have read it put it in the fire.

Your father and I have been talking lately about his debts in England, and have concluded, as soon as gold is at par, to pay them without the interest. Will you ask Mr. Ward to send the acct. and he shall be paid if no one else is, but I have saved nearly enough to pay everyone myself, out of my housekeeping money, which I have out at interest, nearly three hundred pounds, and that, as far as I know, would pay every one off, but your father is able to do it himself, when gold is down.

Your aunt is a great comfort to me, for I should be very lonely now that they have all left but Fred and Robert. She has better health, and an excellent appetite, she enjoys herself much.

Give my love to Polly, and all the other dear children. Tell them about their grandmother. I hope to see them sometime. Train them up in the fear of the Lord. I have no doubt you will. Good bye, my dear children.

Your affect. mother

Ann Cluett

Write a long letter to me, and I will answer it.
Good-bye, good bye.

[Emily's 8th child, Clara, was born in 1864 ("8th difficulty"); therefore this letter was probably written in 1864 or early 1865.]

[The following poem, also undated, could be the "verses for your amusement" that Ann mentions.]

If ever parting pang were felt
That pang was felt by me.
And though the stroke in love was delt
'Twas hard to part from thee.
Thou too didst keenly feel the smart,
How keenly none can know
Else why should sorrow fill thy heart,
Or tears so freely flow.
None but a mother ever knew
What mothers love can be.
Then thou who art a mother too
Will sympathize with me.
Tell me, ye sages, tell me why
This bitter cup was sent.
If 'tis my Fathers will I'll try
To bare in meek content.
Farewell my child, we part once more
The tenderest ties are riven,
But hope to meet again before
We meet in yonder heaven.

Your Affectionate mother,

Ann Cluett

Letter #30 – Ann to son-in-law John Cadby

Newly transcribed partial-letter, by M.C.S., 2021. This is the middle four pages of a letter at the Hart Cluett Museum. The rest is missing.

This note constitutes Ann Cluett's longest exposition urging John Cadby to bring his family to Troy. The theme of encouraging Emily and family to migrate recurs many times in the letters; their genuine desire for this is overlaid here by Ann's multiple attempts to manipulate John into making the decision to come. Most sad is Ann's supposition that John might die in a few years and leave his family; in fact, it was Emily who died, and John who later migrated without her.

October 1864

[p. 5]

…a distant land, not knowing whether she should see their faces more. Only those who have met their ----- providence and whose hearts have been fixed ----- by its inflections ----- can truly understand its devastating ----- And she has been patiently and unmurmuringly [?] waiting and watching for 14 long years for some gleam of light to indicate that a way was opening for a reunion with the much loved and much loving friends of her infancy and youth. It is the wise man who realizes that "hope deferred maketh the heart sick", speaks truly, what heart sickness she must have suffered! as that large reserve of happiness, usually drawn from constant association with parents, brothers, and sisters, has been lost to her for 14 long years. I often think how her heart must have been drawn across the great deep, by those mysterious cords, which invariably unite every family which, like ours, "think and speak the same." How often she has said in her heart "oh that I had wings of the dove." Suns have risen and set, moons have waxed and waned – spring, summer, autumn & winter have succeeded each other – but the re-union thirsted for as "thirsts the hart for cooling streams" has not been realized. But the hope of this reunion has cheered her through days & weeks & seasons & years. Good – for when hope deserts the human soul, then despair enters in and takes possession. In addition to this restoration of a great lost happiness, her precious face in our midst, would relieve her of no inconsiderate portion of that weight of responsibility and care, which she cannot but feel, as the mother of so large a family. Here are friends, both able and willing, to assist her in leading those young minds "in the way they should go", who would share the responsibility, and feel the labor to be only a labor of love. In this connection I may mention what, perhaps, you already know, that Joseph prepares to ----- Johnny for the ministry, which according to my estimate, is a consideration which should have some weight in influencing you in this direction. If, by the providence of God, you should be taken away from them in the course of three or four or more years, who is there in England that would care for them and feel identified with their welfare, as your friends would here? Emily would sink under the accumulated weight of sorrow and responsibility, without some suitable friend to sympathize with her in her grief, or share the heavy burden pressing her to the earth.

------------------- I will now ----- to a few of the reasons which I placed in the other scale, & which I suppose to exert an influence in keeping you at home. And first, you may probably fear that the important step will not influence your condition. We think and believe otherwise, or we would not advise the step to be taken. We think we know you, and we are sure that observation and experience have enabled us to form a tolerably correct estimate of the advantages this country offers to men of your stamp. Unless you should change, the change of country cannot very well fail of resulting in great advantage to you. In England comparatively few men rise above the condition in which they were born. Here, every industrious, careful man rises. Nearly all the rich men in the city have been the architects of their own fortunes. On this head, I will only say further, if this fear be one of your reason, "give to the winds your fear." Another reason of your wishing to remain in England, I have supposed to be the expectation of coming into possession of a portion of your Uncle's property at his death. How large a "portion" this may be, I suppose no means of determining, nor can I form any opinion as to how assured your prospects are, or how long a time may pass before you enter into "possession", but I do think delaying your coming till after your Uncle's death, you may lose four times as much as you will gain by that event. You would be not a little surprised to know how much many business men realize in a single year, in this country. I think you can carve out for yourself a better "inheritance" on this side the water, than you will ever receive by "will." But after all, you must be the best judge of whether the --------------- in view, is worth the sacrifice of years to gain it. I think it is not, but possibly its value may be such, that I may be mistaken on this front. Another reason I have supposed to weigh against your coming is the difficulty you may find in making a profitable disposition of your stock. But looking at it from my stand-point, I do not predict any difficulties that need block your way. I believe your lease expires on the 25th of March next, you have, therefore, nearly 5 months to sell it off. I suppose you can sell a large portion of it at retail, if you make it public that you are relinquishing the business, and offering it at reduced prices. Other portions you could sell at auction, when in Birmingham or in London, as your best judgment may determine. And if you brought a few cases of your best books to

New York, or Troy, they would sell well. Gold is so high, that the importers of English books cannot afford to import them any longer. Thus it seems to me, if you desire to come, the store need not be an obstacle of sufficient magnitude to prevent you. I have thought that probably the most potent [?] reason for your delay is found in (as you may think) the impossibility of leaving your Mother. But is it absolutely necessary that you should leave her behind? Why not bring her along with you? I understand she is healthy, and the voyage may add years to her life. But perhaps you will meet me here with the assurance that "she will not leave England". While I am disposed to consider this as the strongest reason yet put in the scale, against your coming, I am very far from admitting that it is an all-sufficient answer, & closes the question. I would not... [rest of letter missing]

[Ann Cluett]

Letter #31 – Brother George to Emily

In November of 1864, George comments on the price of gold to Emily (then at its wartime high) when considering a trans-Atlantic trip to see her family. Over the course of the Civil War, gold had increased in value from a yearly price of $20.67 USD, to a peak in 1864 of $47.02 USD. To travel would mean losing money on the exchange of gold, and he decides to wait.

Meanwhile, George has paid for a substitute to fight in his place in the war. *"It cost me $500 but clears me for three years."* The Cluetts are now well off. And while George is prospering enough to pay the hefty sum of $500 for a replacement (roughly one year of white collar salary), he is careful with his money and avoids travel when gold is high.

As George says to Emily and John, *"I tell you dear Bro and Sister that if you had come to America when we did you would be rich today...."*

From the perspective of his faith, George laments the recent loss of his wife and greatly anticipated newborn child, while consoling himself with things eternal. *"... if not for the hope I have of meeting those dear ones in a better land, my future should indeed be dark, but... I feel that this light affliction... will work for me a far more exceeding and eternal weight of glory, while I look not at the things that are seen but at the things that are not seen."*

The faith of the Cluetts is genuine and compelling.

Troy Nov 14th 1864

My dear Emily

Your kind letter was rec'd and I cannot tell you how glad I was to hear from you, especially at this time. I assure you, it was more acceptable than you could imagine, and I feel greatly indebted to you for all the real heartfelt sympathy you expressed in my behalf. O how I wish I could see you and talk with you even if it were but for a few moments. I have so much that I would like to tell you, nothing in this wide world would give me greater pleasure than to be in your midst, it seems as if I should really be happy if I could take two or three of you dear little ones upon my knee and converse with them. My dear Sister you do not know how passionately fond I am of little children. And I have wished many and many a time since my bereavement that I had Polly or Emmy or any of them with me. What a comfort it would be to me; I have thought much about coming to see you for some time past and I would start at once but it does seem as though it would be very extravagant for us to take such a trip with gold at 240. Nothing but this prevents my coming, for my business is very quiet just at present, so that this is the only thing that stands in my way, I assure you. If gold were at 150 you would see me in Birm' in three weeks time. I have made up my mind to come and see you just as soon as the way seems clear, but must postpone it for the present. I feel very grateful to you and my dear brother John for your very kind invitation, and I do not wish you to consider that I decline its acceptance, but merely "lay it on the table" for a little while, hoping that the time is not too far distant when I shall be with you -----

I think of you a great deal, and when I contrast my condition with yours I wonder why it is that I am left thus alone, truly you are favored! And yet I should not say that I am alone for God has been very near and precious to me in my affliction and great and terrible as it has been I have been able to look up to Him and say "Thy will be done" and if not for the hope I have of meeting those dear ones in a better land, my future should indeed be dark, but it is all well, I feel that this light affliction which is but for a moment, will work for me a far more exceeding and eternal weight of glory, while I look not at the things which are seen, but at the things which are not seen ----- no one could be more delightfully situated than I was but four short months ago, a beautiful home and a wife who well deserved all the love I bestowed upon her, one who well understood how to make home happy ----- and then we looked forward with delight to the time when another would be added to our little family circle. How vain were all my hopes and anticipations! The house which I had built for Sarah but which we had enjoyed but six months of our married life, is now empty, the family altar ground which we had so often knelt to thank our heavenly Father for the many blessings we enjoyed and where you too were often been remembered, is broken up ----- Surely God moves in a mysterious way. But, Emily, sad and afflicting are these providences I have very much even more for which to be thankful,

I presume Mary has informed you that I am living with her, I assure you a better home I could not have, unless it were my old home. They all do everything in their power to make me happy and I am sure I appreciate it highly. Joseph is one of my very best brothers, he is truly good and I enjoy his society very much, I think that none of the Cluett family have married more happily than Mary and she well deserves a good husband. We sing together now as in former years and as we are both fond of music, we spend many pleasant hours in this way, indeed I do not know what I would do without it.

It does seem too bad that you were separated from us so, we have so many delightful family meetings. How much more we should enjoy them if you were all with us. Why is it that you cannot make up your mind to come to America? Tell John that if he holds out much longer I intend to come over and take you all by force of arms. I tell you my dear Bro and Sister that if you had come to

America when we did you would be rich today, but I suppose it is useless for me to tell you what father has told you so often before; I have no doubt that when the right time comes you will start, and I trust that time is not far off. To be sure things in this country have not looked quite as prosperous of late, but I assure you this is but temporary, I feel confident that this war will not last much longer, our enemy is well nigh exhausted, President Lincoln has again been elected by a large majority to govern us for another four years, which is in itself a great victory and will do much to dishearten the Rebels, it will be utterly impossible for them to resist the power of our government much longer. You can imagine how their money has depreciated when I tell you that it takes sixty dollars to buy a pair of children's shoes! What do you think of that? The war goes on successfully, and I have not the least doubt as to the ability of our government to put down this terrible rebellion. Some time ago I was drafted but as my name was almost the last on the list and the city being credited with more men, my name was dropped, so I did not have to turn soldier, but I am ready to go whenever it becomes necessary. I sent a substitute a few months ago to fight for me, it cost me $500 ----- but clears me for three years, so I see but little chance of my becoming a Major Gen.

I am very much pleased with the letters Polly writes to her Aunt Mary, they are very prettily written for one so young. I hope she will write one to me sometime, I think a great deal of Polly, I have a large picture of her hanging by the side of my bed. I recollect well when I took her to have it taken just before she left us. I sat in the Picture Gallery with her and I was talking to her about leaving me, the tears trickled down her cheeks. I was very sorry to part with her, tell her I hope she will always be a good girl, indeed if I ever come to see you, you must make up your mind to part with one of the children for I do not intend to depart alone, so this must be thoroughly understood before hand so that we have no misunderstanding about the matter. I really believe if I had such a family as you have I should be the proudest man in Troy.

You asked me to give you what information I could in regard to the cause of Sarah's death ----- She was taken sick early on Friday morn July 29th, I went for the doctor at 5 o'clock, he came and thought everything was going right. Her pains kept increasing until ten or eleven o'clock when they began to decrease and she said she was very tired and seemed much exausted. Her [Mother ?] asked the doctor if he could not give her something to increase the pain and assist in expelling the child, he then gave her tincture of Ergot which increased her pain but in about fifteen minutes she went into a violent spasm. I went immediately for one of our best physicians who brought his instruments with him which he used and the child was born in a few minutes or about 20 minutes to one o'clock. Her sufferings were frightful in the extreme, her screams being heard for some distance. I trust I never shall witness another such scene as long as I live. I never shall forget it. I had not anticipated the least difficulty, her health had been extremely good until within one week of her confinement. The spasms continued at intervals until ½ past seven Oclk Saturday night when they ceased and she remained in sort of a stupor until Sunday morning about 9 Oclk. I went to her bedside and asked her if she knew me, she said "Why yes", as plainly as she could for she had bitten her tongue badly in her convulsions. I then asked her to kiss me which she did, from this time she began to fail and never spoke to me again. She died on Monday morning August 1st without a struggle. The doctor said her death was caused by the Albuminous condition of the urine which he said caused her weakness and inability to expel the child, but I cannot rid myself of the idea that the Ergot caused her death. I should like to have your opinion upon this matter much, you have had a good deal of experience in these matters. I should like to know what you think about it.

For now I shall have to close for I do not like crossed letters. I hope you will write to me again soon, you would if you knew how much good a letter from you does me. All the family are about as well as usual. Please do tell the children that their Uncle George thinks a great deal of them all and wants them all to be good and love God. Kiss them all for me.

with love to John and yourself I remain
Your affectionate brother

George

In this letter George has made plain both his love of children, and his genuine wish to bring some of Emily's children to America, which he and his second wife Amanda later do.

George's mention here of "*crossed letters*" refers to the practice of writing a letter, then rotating the paper ninety degrees and writing perpendicularly over top of existing text in order to save paper.

Letter #32 – Mary to Emily

In May of 1865, Mary writes to Emily, "*Ma wishes you to gather in Father's accounts and send them to him for as gold is going down so rapidly we hope soon to have them settled; Mr. Ward's included. What a glorious day that will be to all of us!*"

They are still bothered by their debt to their friend Mr. Ward. However, after Ann mentioned in a letter a year earlier that Mr. Ward had still not been repaid, they have yet to repay him. The entire family has been aware of the money owing during the fifteen years they have lived in Troy, and Mary clearly feels the moral weight of the overdue obligations.

As for how they are doing financially, "*Father is being prospered in the business and is now having fitted up another store opening into his with handsome plate glass windows for his pianos. He is doing well.*"

In this letter we hear the only reference to a child that the Mulfords spontaneously decided to bring into their home. Evidently they did not keep this child, as she is never again referred to in correspondence or other family and public records.

The Civil War has ended and "*Slavery is abolished. Ah the hand of God has overruled for our own good.*"

Troy May 8th 1865

My dear Emily,

For weeks I have waited to hear from you. Why am I not relieved from my intense anxiety about you. In your silence I imagine all sorts of sad things transpiring in your household. I am, I know, blamable for not writing sooner, but still, as each day seemed so filled up [with] all sorts of engagements, I would hope that tomorrow might bring a respite, but no, I find that cares increase and I must not look for any cessation of labor here. Years ago, I used to think I was busy, but with all the little various engagements of a rector's wife, I seem doubly busy.

I have now so much to say, I hardly know where to begin, but I suppose you would like to know something of our little daughter. We think she is a fine child, large, plump, and apparently healthy. When she came I thought she resembled Annie more than any child I ever saw; she has beautiful eyes, red cheeks, and white teeth. She feels perfectly at home and says "Mama, "Papa" very nicely. Do you think we were foolish? Well, we had a pleasant home and wanted some poor homeless child to share it with us. We are not at all disappointed in her, and it does me good to see Joseph so fond of her. He jumps about with her after his hard study, like a little boy. You would have laughed to see the bustle in our house after she came, for of course there had been no preparation for her and she was almost destitute of clothing. Ma and Aunt made a coat of brown and white plaid [?], trimmed the cape with fringe and Aunt made a beautiful little bonnet of blue satin. Then a rocking chair had to be bought; and a crib which stands near my bedside. Ma is very much pleased with her, indeed Ma was so struck with her appearance that she was desirous that we should take her. Of course it gives me more to do, but the love she brings with her is more than recompense. She has a very stubborn will and Ma thinks I have at last found my match. The thing that I am glad of, is that Joseph and I agree perfectly on the training she is to receive, as we do on every matter of importance.

I am all alone tonight; Joseph has gone to a meeting, George has gone to a teacher's meeting and Mother is in Phila. [Philadelphia] where she has been for a week past. We expect her home this week, and if she comes, Joseph and I will start on [that ?] day for our old parish, and shall hope to remain in Phila. about two weeks. I shall be glad to go, for Joseph is really worn down with his labors for the past two months. Really, I see very little of him, for after morning prayer he goes to his study; after dinner he goes out to talk to his people on the subject of religion. And after tea we have singing, reading Jay's devotions and prayer, then Joseph starts out again on the same errand and so his evenings are spent. I am thankful that there is much religious interest in the church and next Sunday a large number will be added to our membership. We are to have a new church next Spring. My bible class continues very interesting, with constant additions.

I suppose Jodie Mattice will not be with us longer than next week as Edmund expects to get into his house then, but poor boy, he cannot have much comfort for Mary [Mary Mattice, Edmund's first wife, died a month after this letter] is so sickly that she can do nothing. She lies down most of the day and coughs incessantly and so ------ that she destroys the happiness of all about her. Ma and Aunt are weary of her and Edmund has no comfort in her society. She quarrels with her sisters and little Jodie, in fact with everybody. She is selfish and exacting, and yet to visitors she is as lovely as an angel. You may judge of her supreme selfishness when she said once of her little brother who is thrown entirely on her kindness, she " wasn't going to take care of other people's young ones"! Jodie says he wishes he could stay with us for Mary is so cross. Edmund has told her she may not live six months, but that makes her no better. He says he should have left her if he had not been surrounded by friends. I am truly sorry for her, she seems so possessed by an evil spirit that she can take no advice. I have talked to her how Joseph and I live and entreating her earnestly to adopt the same method, but all to no purpose; she says the men are selfish, domineering, etc. Oh I do pity them both for they take no pleasure in each others society. I should be thankful if she were prepared for her departure, and then that event would be hailed with delight by all, Edmund included. Isn't that a fearful picture of married life?

Alfred has moved into his house, and I think enjoys married life much. Lillie will be confined very shortly. I wish you could see how pleasantly they are situated.

I made my daily visit to Ma's this afternoon. She has been ill in bed for more than a week, but is better so she thinks she will get up tomorrow. Indeed I do not want to go away and leave her in bed. Aunt is quite low spirited as her mind dwells on the scenes of a year ago. Ah! How well I remember my feeling a year since; with what anxiety I looked forward to my married life; but now I can look back with thankfulness upon the past year and say it was all right; God was directing me.

May 11th. It is raining very heavily. George is sitting in the study read'g the paper, Joseph is writing a sermon. I wish you could see how snug we are. I was up on the hill this afternoon. Ma is still in bed very weak and poorly. I am going in the morning to try to get her into another room, and when she is able, she is to come and stay a while with us for change of scene. Aunt is better, but very anxious to hear from you and John Lewis. Has any information been gained of Margaret's whereabouts? Ma wishes you to collect and gather in Father's accounts and send them to him for as gold is going down so rapidly we hope soon to have them settled. Mr. Ward's included. What a glorious day that-----be to us all!

Father is being prospered in the business and is now having fitted up another store opening into his with handsome plate glass windows for his pianos. He is doing well. What do you think of our country? How strange the war is ended. How thankful I am that it is so and that Slavery is abolished. Ah the hand of God has overruled for our own good.

How is you dear little baby? [Clara was born in 1865.] I fear you will be worn down by care which I would share if I were near you. Will that time ever come? I love to think of you and the family and often wish ardently to be with you again.

Phil. 16th. I did not have time to finish my letter to you before leaving home so, on this morning after my ---------- I will try to post it or it will not go by tomorrow's mail. Your long looked for letter came a few days ago. I was thankful for it, but felt very sorrowful after perusing it. Oh! Emily you have too much to do and I wish I could help you. I will try to write again after I get home which will be the week after next and then I will answer you letter. I am sitting in Dr. Newton's study while Joseph is writing to his Mother, and Alfred (who has been here since Sat) writing to Lillie. I wish you could see us. I left Ma better although I think she tried to be as well as she could be for my sake. She knew how badly I should have felt to leave her ill. Ed. had just gotten possession of his home which he says he is furnishing to be miserable. Ah, that is a living trouble to him. He wants to go to England and he says he would if Mary were likely to live.

Oh I wish I was with you! Can't you keep John out of Babone's company? I never could bear to see them together; but more anon.

Your loving sister,

Mary

Letter #33 – Mary to Emily

This letter follows Emily's only visit to America when she was reunited, for a short while, with her family.

Troy Jan 3rd 1866

My dearest Emily.

When you left us I had no idea that so much time would elapse before my writing to you, but really I have been so hurried with the Fair preparations, that my mind has been constantly over tasked. Your letters came to hand in due time and it gave us all pleasure to know you were safe in your own home. How strange everything connected with your trip must now seem to you! Well, we all feel sure your whole family will be here by and bye. Although I know you would rather receive letters from the boys, I am really compelled to take their places this time, for they have been, and now are, so busy taking account of stock, they are worn out. George and Edmund did not get to bed till three o'clock this morning.

Ma is about the same; she and Aunt sit and bear each other company. Indeed I think anything connected with our family is as you left us except the great event of the season – Fred's wedding, and it is in reference to this I write in much haste. His health you know is very poor, and Mr. Bishop has determined to pay his expenses in taking a Continental tour as soon as they are married; and Mr. Bishop wishes Fred, if his health improves, to travel through Europe until it is established, even for six months. They will be married on Thursday the 11th and leave New York in the "City of

London" on the 13th. They intend spending a few days in Birm. but will 'put up' at the "Hen and Chickens". Ma wishes them to come right to your house but I urged that they should engage a hotel first. Did I do right? I thought that although you would wish them to be with you, the trouble consequent upon their staying nights with you would be too much for you. I should like John to meet them at the Birm. Station if he finds out when the vessel is in. I need not tell you of the splendid affair, as I suppose Fannie, when she sees you can tell you more than I can. Wonders will never cease! Who thought when you left that they would so soon follow you? Oh I wish I could be with you a little while. Do you think John will come soon? Ask him to return with Fred and Fannie. Give my love to him and all the dear little children.

I am in a great hurry this afternoon. Will you write to me soon? I want to know how you found your home all right and in good order and all about the children's delight on your return. Ma feels as though you would all come soon. Will she be mistaken? We have had accounts of the impurity of the English atmosphere. Perhaps that will drive you here. – well until then, I am

ever

Your affect'ate sister

Mary

Letter #34 – Ann to Emily

Ann writes to Emily in April of 1867. Ann describes the family grief at the loss of Alfred's first-born, son Robbie.

With respect to the debts, Ann says, *"To think Mr. Ward is gone! I shall send his widow the money."* Despite Ann avowing three years earlier (in 1864) that Mr. Ward would be paid *"if no one else is"*, and reiterating this in 1865, he still has not been remunerated. This suggests the other creditors (those in a lower priority than Mr. Ward) were not paid yet either.

Troy April 1867

My dear Emily,

I promised you a long letter some time ago, but I have, since that time, been so poorly I did not feel able. I am a little better now. We have lately had to pass throug a severe trial in the loss of our dear little Robbie, you can form an idea what delight that child offered us all. How he made us forget trouble, and sickness, and, I was going to say, almost everything else. Your father was very fond of him, I never thought he would of greived so about him. He often says he does not know how to be reconciled to the loss. I feared, at the time, it would nearly crush Alfred to the earth, and indeed it does almost at times, though he feels nothing contrary to the will of God. We all do everything we can to comfort him and poor Lillie. Lillie expects to be confined early in July.

You say John works too hard. I know he cannot help it in his business, and then he has so large a family to provide for, it must require the exercise (to its utmost capability) of every nerve and fiber of both body and mind to keep up steam enough to run such ponderous machinery. And if there is not reserve sufficient to keep up a continual supply of material to create that steam what will the end be? I wish you were all here, but I would not lift up my finger to persuade John to come. We all think that when he sees it his duty to come then he will come, and we do not want him to think we are over anxious about the matter, nor do we want you to think that you are cut off from your family by any means, but on the contrary, we intend for our correspondence to be more frequent than it has yet been, and a feeling of sympathy kept up, more in time, and fervent than ever.

I think your father has mentioned in his letter the probable coming of Fred and Fanny to your shores again. Fred's health is so bad that he scarcely knows what to do, and he thinks that another voyage would help him, and it is possible they may come this summer, if they do they will write and let you know all about it. How fast people are passing away! To think Mr. Ward is gone! We were all astonished to hear it. I am sorry. He will be missed, both in his family, his church, and the community. I shall send his widow the money.

Fred's baby is about the prettiest little fellow I ever saw, he is as round and as plump as a little cupid. The great grandmother has charge of him, I seldom see him, we live so far off. I know not whether any of them have told you about Edmund or not, however I will just say that he had his lady have parted, she proved fickle and disappointed him. He felt rather badly about it for a few days, then concluded, with our persuasions, that such a girl was not worth regretting, or grieving over. He is going to occupy the house he bought, having rented the upper part to a family who will board him, and a young man who is going to live with him. He will furnish the two parlors elegantly, better, even than if he had married. The young man who is going to live with him has also been disappointed in love, so they are going to console each other, and speak against all the girls in creation. I am very glad he missed Clara, for I think she would have been very domineering.

George will be married about the middle of June. He has bought a house joining our garden, will have possession of it the first of May, but it will take three months to complete the improvements he will make upon it, and he and his wife are coming to live with us till his house is ready. Mrs. Mulford is still with us, she sends her love to you.

Your aunts health is still very poor, she wishes me to say that she will write to you when she is better, and tell you the truth, the whole truth, and nothing but the truth. She is quite contented now, and is sorry she ever said anything to give you the impression that she wanted to come back, last autumn she did talk of it, her health was so much worse, but when the Doctor told her what her complaint was, and that there was no cure for it, (she thinking before that, that another voyage would cure her) she felt perfectly satisfied yes very thankful that she was where she could be taken care of. She sends her love to John, and thanks him for sending her the papers, she says how pleasant it is to be so kindly remembered by him.

I am glad to here that Pollie, Emmie, and Lizzie are so industrious, and are becoming so useful to you. What would I not give if I could step in some day and see you in your nice country home! I do not feel so far from you as I used, so many are going, and coming, and the voyage are made so quick that the distances seem to diminish, and if I was able I should soon make you a visit. I want you, my dear child, to feel perfectly happy and contented, as I know you will, and the time will come, I have faith to believe, when we shall meet again on this side the water.

A Cluett

It becomes clear through reading the letters that William and Ann had pushed off repayment of many of their debts for seventeen years. If, despite their rapid economic progress and eventual social and business success, they never did pay an individual they felt particularly beholden to, it is possible that some debts were never repaid.

Letter #35 – William to Emily

In this letter William indicates they are 'out of the book selling business', a part of their business that William held onto for a long time (since 1856 when he introduced pianos), despite "*pianos pay*[ing] *better*".

Troy April 15, 1867

My Dear Daughter

Your welcome letter was handed to me yesterday afternoon. It is nearly ½ past 8 oClock in the evening, & I have just returned from the store. The present seems to present as good an opportunity as any I can hope to have, to write a line or two. Your letter was not calculated to excite very pleasing emotions, but on the contrary, to add to the very great regret I feel (in common with the rest of the family), that you did not come to us years ago. I fear John will sink under the great burden laid upon him. I can easily understand how his incessant toil must pile upon him. And if his health should prematurely give way!! I know of no one just now that seems to me to need so strong a confidence in God, as you do. It is easy to believe in noon day light, but in the thick & impenetrable darkness, it is altogether different.

With such a family, your expenses must inevitably increase, & an increasingly profitable business is therefore absolutely necessary. I know it to be much more difficult to enlarge a business in England than it is in America. But we must believe that "the Lord will provide".

Many changes have taken place since I wrote my last letter. We are [out of ?] the Bookselling, Stationery, & Sheet Music business, & our stock is nearly sold off. It seemed a great sacrifice to throw so good a business away, after it had cost us so many years toil, & so many thousands of Dollars to establish it. But we found when we came to take stock at the beginning of the year, that the Piano business had paid us best, though it had not received scarcely a tenth part of the time & labor devoted to the Books, tc. [etc.] How we all wished that John had been here to take to the whole concern as it stood! But we knew it would be of no avail to inform him of our purpose. For myself, I must confess, I have very small hope of ever seeing the family in this country. Before many years, the elder children will be forming life connections, & then farewell to every prospect & hope of immigration. The reason I have stated is not the only one that influenced us to give up our miscellaneous trade. A second was the fact that Fred's declining health warned us that we could not count very long upon his aid, & as 5 of us were not sufficient to meet the demands of the growing business, we felt sure it would be much worse for us when Fred's help was withdrawn. He & Fanny will probably visit you next month. A third reason for this change, was the close, incessant attention & labor required from me in keeping all the wheels of the machine in motion. For the last 2 years especially, I have worked, as they say "like a slave". I have travelled 2 & 3 nights in a week in the Cars [?] to save the precious day time, & frequently when in the store have not sat down through the whole day, except at meals. And the children thought it was about time for me to take things a little more easy, & I began to think & feel so too. Not that the Piano Forte & Organ business is going to be run without attention & labor, but it will be a much more agreeable business, & will not shut us up so many hours a day.

Your Mamma's health has not been very good but she is better now. We had a very delightful drive this afternoon, & it seemed to do her much good. The weather has been so rough & cold that riding much for pleasure has been out of the question. I think when she can go out every day, she will improve rapidly. Your Aunt Lewis' health is rather poor. She is almost constantly in trouble with her bowels, or stomach, or back. I fear she will never be very strong. Mary has been very poorly the last week or two. She is laboring about as much to shorten her life as the wife of a minister, as she did as a Music Teacher. They have begun the work of enlarging & beautifying the Church, & before the work is completed, she will be in the "Church above" unless she desists from her exhausting labor. I have filled my sheet. Best love to John & Polly & all the rest. Wish Aunt Reed [?] well.

Your aff Father

W. C.

Letter #36 – Mary to Emily

It is nineteen months later. Emily now has ten children. Robert has married Lizzie (Elizabeth Marchisi), and she is about to be 'confined' as she is pregnant.

Mary remarks that she thinks Emily (with ten children) might not be as busy as she (Mary) is, as a minister's wife. This reflects a Cluett family tendency in these letters to underestimate the challenges facing Emily and her husband, John, from early on.

Troy N.Y. Nov 2nd 1868

My dear Emily,

I fear you are angry with me for not writing sooner, but perhaps you would think me less to blame if you knew how I was situated. In the first place we moved from the country, then I went to N.Y. and then to Boston, and Joseph has been away twice on church business, and part of the time I closed the house and stayed at Ma's. Now I am at home my time has been taken up with calling and receiving calls that I sometimes hardly know what to do. Then again Joseph's Mother has been very ill with a serious attack of Pleurisy. She was taken ill at Ma's so of course I had to be there all the time except at mealtimes. Her health is not very good any time but she is rather better now.

Ma had a letter from you a few days since announcing the birth of your little girl. How thankful we are to know of your moving! You must have been very weak to need ergot [?]. Much as I admire large families I hope you will have no more; indeed I do not know how you can manage with ten children. Sometimes however, I think your work is not as arduous as mine, for you can stay at home and not feel responsible to a whole congregation. I am glad to hear the children are thinking of living a religious life, and I do wish Johnny or Polly or Emmie or Annie would write to me all about it. The other day at dinner Joseph and I were talking about you, and it seemed then as though I would overleap every obstacle to be once more in your family circle. He was saying how much he would like to travel next summer, and then he planned that we should both visit you and I stay with you while he went on the Continent. How would John like that? Would he leave home or would he be reconciled to us? Of course I dare not expect to come, but in the event of doing so I want to know how I should be received.

Ma is tolerably well for her. Aunt is very poorly all the time. She took the news of John's death very hard indeed; it made her so ill that she kept her bed for some time after. I was very sorry she mourned so, for I know he would have hardly given his Mother's death a second thought. She was very glad of that letter you sent her and she told me to thank you for it. Ma is very happy with her family on both sides of her. She enjoys walking around the gardens and popping into each house. I wish you could know Amanda, she is one of the sweetest dispositions I ever saw. I know you would love her very much. We also like Lizzie, she is pleasant and very desirous of pleasing. Robert is quite happy in his home. I suppose Lizzie will be confined as soon as is proper.

Lillie is all over her illness and has a remarkably fine boy, over whom there was great rejoicing. He looks strong enough to eat beef-steak. The two little twins are lovely, they are sensible looking and very loveable. Now what shall I say of Fred? Why that I think he has just about as much trouble with Fanny as he ever had. He will say nothing concerning her except that she is kind and good, but she hates his family and often degrades him before company calling him mean and all sorts of things. This summer we went away with Robert and Lizzie but Fannie contrived to take all pleasure away from the party. Afterward they went to Canada with George and Amanda and there she behaved just as badly as she could behave, so that Fred threatened to leave her, but after all he did not want anything said about it at home. So he has to live. Oh dear what a horrid piece of humanity. She is always accusing him of not getting anything for her, and yet he works and -------- ------- all he has on her and must be a poor man. You must not tell him what I have written for he would be angry I have no doubt.

Father works just as hard as ever he did. He travels a great deal, indeed he is hardly ever at home; his health is quite good. Edmund lives in Albany, has his parlor and bedroom and keeps bachelor's hall. Until lately he has taken his meals at a hotel paying the enormous price of nearly three pounds a week. He however has found out that it is too dear so he boards himself. He gets up in the morning and cooks mutton chop sweet potatoes and coffee, and he enjoys it more than if it was prepared for him.

Joseph is much better than he has been for a long time and is getting fat. I am so glad you speak so well of John as a husband, it is very delightful when passing years only serve to strengthen the affection existing between man and wife. For my own part I often wonder whether anyone has a better husband than I have, for he is kind and attentive, and thoughtful of my comfort. He always likes to hear from you and says he wishes you would come again. When will that time be? I cannot be reconciled to the thought that your children will marry in England and therefore have all their interests there away from us. They must come to settle here; we must not be separated all our lives. How I wish you would send Annie over to me. I would promise to take great care of her.

I believe I have not spoken of Alfred. He is quite well and in good spirits. Their business is very good. We have some friends passing through Birm. soon. You remember Mrs. Francis; the whole family expect shortly to spend a year in Europe, so we may have an opportunity of sending you a little parcel. I'll not wait to write any more for I want this to go off this evening. So goodbye my dear dear Sister.

Mary

Mrs. Mulford wishes me to give her love to you.
Please write very soon.

Letter #37 – Emily to George

Despite the fact that this set of correspondence contains forty-three letters between Emily and the Cluett family, only six of the letters are from Emily — two in 1850, and four in 1869. In this letter we have a glimpse of some of the challenges that faced Emily and John Cadby, when Emily says to George, *"You did a 'big thing' when you offered to take two of the children* [to America] *free of expense..."*

July 15, 1869

My Dear George

You did a "big thing" when you offered to take two of the children free of expense, & it has been the subject of conversation ever since. A few days before, Pollie was trying to persuade John to let them go, but he made the excuse that he could not afford it. Now you have removed that difficulty, & I think John is half inclined to let them go, but I am afraid to raise your expectations lest he should again change his mind. Supposing they should go, the question arises, can their berths be secured bye & bye? I am afraid to take [tell ?] them yet, still it would not be amiss perhaps, if you wrote to them enquiring what would be the fares for three of their ages.

I want to see you to talk it over with you. I do not know how I can part with my children in such a sweeping way as that would be, although I believe it would be for their good. I cannot say half what I want to say must leave it till I see you. Write soon & say when that will be.

With much love to Amanda,

I remain your loving
Sister

Emily

Letter #38 – Mary to Emily

Mary, as do the rest of the Cluett family members, yearns to see Emily's children. She hears some of the children may come to Troy but she doesn't dare have her hopes raised until she has "*ocular demonstration*"; this phrase a characteristic example of the family love of words and word play. Mary comments in this letter on Fred's wife Fannie, and their son's responses to her.

Troy, Aug. 9th 1869

My dear Emily,

I have had no letter from you for sometime, but I feel like penning a few lines this afternoon. You must be enjoying yourself intensely, and indeed as long as you have company and so much engrossed in them, I cannot expect you to write. When they have left, and all has settled into its own routine I wish you would talk to me a great deal through your pen, and tell me everything in connection with their visit. Are you intending to send any of the children? George says so, but I cannot believe it. Ma often says "when Pollie comes", but I at once try not to have her build such air castles. You know how glad we shall be to see them, but as I have been disappointed once, I shall not allow myself to think anything about it until I have ocular demonstration. George says yours is a splendid family. When will you all be with us? Ma is sitting by me reading the newspaper, waiting for Father to take her to ride. She is very much better than she was a few months since for she takes the air every day for about two hours. Poor Fred has the worst times. He looks as if he had no hope left. Such a thin, sorrowful looking man you may rarely see. Fannie is no better judge than she ever was. At her best she is simply ridiculous, and at her worst she is ready for the lunatic asylum. One day a short time since she and Fred had trouble at Ma's while little Freddie was by. He said nothing then, but afterwards when she was again bringing him up the steps he said, "Ma, don't say any more words." Another day he said to his Father "What a funny Ma I've got. I don't love Ma". Isn't it sad to think of all the harsh words he is destined to hear as long as he lives. I do pity Fred from the bottom of my heart. He would very much like to go away without Fannie so that his spirits may revive, but no she will not let him do so on any consideration, so I suppose he will try to form a party and leave sometime this week. Truly a wife has it in her power to make her husband miserable. In thinking over my blessings I cannot but thank God for one the best husband in the world. Oh I cannot see why poor Fred should be so afflicted. All the others have good wives but I think George has the best.

What would I not give to have you for awhile at our country home. Would not we have some cozy chats? Do you know I love the country, and I hope some day when Joseph is unable to preach, we may be able to own a small place away from the dirt and bustle of the city. You do wisely to keep your family in the outskirts of the town. How is your health? Are you quite strong? Tell me all about yourself in you ----- How strange that you and I should be so differently situated. You having a large family and I with none. I should love a large family I am sure, and once I thought I might bring children up, but I love my way of living so much in reading and attending to church matters that I do not feel like repining for a moment. And then Joseph is so weak naturally that I am glad to be able to shield him from all unnecessary pain or trouble. I am now writing in Aunt's room where she lies in bed favoring herself. She says "tell Emily she must send Pollie to take my place for I am going to another". She feels this but I trust she will be spared a long time yet. What are Lizzie and Annie doing? Can one of them write me a letter? How I long to see you all! Give my love to John. If he forgets me I do not forget him. Send me a long letter as soon as you can.

Your loving Sister,

Mary

Your small portrait hangs in Aunt's room, and she says she thinks about you every day. Ma says Father has his flag as high as he can just in expectation of the children coming. You mustn't disappoint him. Ma has a nice bedroom waiting for Pollie and Emmie.

Letter #39 – Emily to George

This letter communicates the sorrow both Emily and her husband John feel after George and Amanda leave with three of the Cadby children en route to Troy; John Jr., Pollie (Mary), and Emmie (Emily).

Birm. Friday Sep 3rd 1869

My dear George

Yesterday was a fearful day, one long to be remembered. I should not care to pass through such another day. I was at the Station when you started though I did not let any of you see me. John & I watched the train till it was out of sight & then we left with heavy hearts. It was getting dark when we reached home at night, & I almost dreaded entering the house. Mary had made a pleasant fire, & the four chairs were placed as usual, seemingly waiting for their accustomed occupants. We neither of us spoke, our hearts were full & we sate down to our lonely meal & ate it in silence. Then we sat in the easy chairs & both went fast asleep. I was the first to wake up & find it ten o'clock. I then roused John & we went to bed with nothing to say, & slept soundly all night. I had several thoughts of winding up the music box, but dare not. This morning we are feeling a little better had finished breakfast by eight oclock, the children asking sundry questions about you. I saw Aunt Radnale yesterday & again today & each time she began to cry. Mr. Smith says on Wednesday night when they got home Aunt said she knew when Emily went she would take her along. "Weeks" [?] fetched some whiskey & they all sat drinking the health of the travellers until a late hour.

George Haliday [?] was in several times in a day, this afternoon he sat down to tea with us, he said he should never think so much of any one again. I have been thinking of you all day wondering what you are all doing, fearing you are all very sick & wishing I could be with you. It has been a pleasant day but I expect you have not been able to enjoy it. I would give something to take a peek at you.

Tell Pollie Miss Wright of Narborne called today to invite her & Emmie to a birthday party. She was amased to find they had left the country. Tell them also that Mrs. Mathas died this morning.

I may now tell you that Johnnie is at liberty to make his home where it is thought best, if Mary should want ----- [the paper is torn]

----- him with her I should like it much.

The Baby is just about the same, only thinner & weaker, she was so glad to see me return home this evening & when I asked her where Uncle & Aunty were, she looked all around in wonder.

Write me very soon & give me a "full, true, & particular" account of your voyage, reception & so on & tell the children to do the same. With many prayers & kisses, I am

Your loving sister

Emily

Sat 6 o'clock. I intended to post this last night but afterwards concluded to come to town tonight & wait to hear from you. I am greatly dissapointed to find there is nothing & fear you are all too ill to write.

John asked Georgie this morning why he did not go with Uncle. He said Uncle never came to put my hat on else I would. John said, you are ----- [the paper is torn] ----- all alone now. He said, & so are you.

I saw by the post of Thursday, you had the "Harvard" Men with you & I learn to day that you were at Queenston at noon of Friday.

This has been a lovely day. I hope you will have such weather all through. You cannot imagine how anxious we feel about you & shall continue to be untill we know you are safe on the other side.

E.C.

Letter #40 – George to John and Emily, en route to America

"City of A", Queenstown Sep 3/69 [1869]

Dear John and Emily

We have arrived safe and sound at the above port, having experienced the most delightful weather thus far; the channel being as smooth as could be desired, the "City of Antwerp" is a fine ship not so large as the "City of London" but much cleaner so altogether we are quite happy and comfortable, Polly and Emmy have good berths and so has John, ours is similar to the one we occupied on the "London". Polly was a little sick last night but the others are quite well, indeed I might say jolly. Thus far they have presented themselves at table as regularly as at home and have "partaken with avidity"; John is quite enthusiastic and is determined to accustom himself to the motion of the vessel! I never saw anyone happier in my life. I was very glad you left us as you did it at the Depot, it was altogether best, the parting was quite severe enough as it was I assure you, for all of us; after the train had got well started we all felt much better; we arrived in L'pool [Liverpool] before 12 o'clock and at 3 o'clock took the tender for the ship, got on board without any trouble and after worrying the steward sometime secured five good seats at table together. So you see we are all right in every respect, all we have to wish now is that Providence will favor us with a safe and speedy voyage across the Atlantic. We feel assured that many prayers are being offered in our behalf on both sides of the water, and have no doubt all will be well. Although we staid with you so long it seems now as though the time was very short and that we had said but little to you. I can never thank you enough for your kindness to both of us, but I shall look forward anxiously to the time when in America I shall be permitted to make some return for your many favors. We all trust you will keep in good spirits, and remember that everything will be done for the comfort and happiness of your children; await with patience the good time which is certainly coming.

John says he shall not be sick for a day or two at any rate. The sun is shining brightly and a gentle breeze blowing; they are all on deck except your

Aff. bro
God bless you all.

Geo [George B. Cluett]

Letter #41 – Emily to George and Amanda

Monday Sep 5, 1869

Dear George & Amanda,

I cannot tell you how glad we were to receive your letter from Queenstown which we did Sunday evening. The news it contained relieved our minds greatly. We were much surprised that John & Emmie had not been sick. I expect by this time you have got out into the ocean & are sick enough. You said nothing of yourselves, so

I suppose you were as well as the rest. I wish I could follow you & know every day what passes amongst you but that cannot be & I must wait anxiously what will seem a long time before I can know any more about you. We have got through our first Sunday alone tolerably well. We did not go to chapel. We scarcely felt equal to sitting in an empty pew to be gazed at, but at 5 o'clock we went to town to see if there were a letter & were amply rewarded for our trouble. After we had read it John said "let us go up & read it to Mother", so we went but she said she did not want to hear anything about them but would rather talk about something else. This morning when I reached the shop a woman had been to say she was taken ill in the night & wished to see us. I went at once & found she had an attack of her old complaint Diarrhea but was much better. We had to send our errand boy home again this morning very sick, so our helps are becoming fewer.

I must tell you John walked into the parlour to dinner in George's gown & slippers, the children were amused & the girls laughed outright, the baby kept glancing at him all the afternoon & then she would turn to me & make one of her funny faces. John came to her & said "let Uncle take the little "Pooslins" for a walk" so she slid off my lap & tried to walk but she could not & came back & laid her head on my shoulder again. She gets no better & I am sure if the cough is to stay all winter she will not stand it.

Harry has gone back to his old situation at W.hampton untill he can hear of something better. The more I know, the more I am satisfied he was waiting an invitation from you. Mr. Stroud left town on Saturday for a week or two, to try if change of scene would divert his mind from the object which had engrossed all thoughts of late. I may be allowed to sympathise with him I guess, now that Pollie is quite out of reach. I can plainly see if she had not gone, that thing would have been inevitable.

Tuesday 7. I am at the shop alone today. John having gone to Lichfield. He is in good spirits, better than I ever supposed he would be. If the children are happy & do well, I do not think we shall wish them back but be glad they are safe there, where I hope after a while to be. I have no doubt John will come at the right time. I am sure from what he says he will not stay from his children when there is an opening in that direction & his Mother no longer stands in the way.

It has been delightful weather since you left. I hope it will hold out another week.

Do not say anymore about favors. We tried to make you comfortable in our rough way, as of course anyone would those they dearly love. I only wish it could have been done better. You showered so many kindnesses upon us that I am sure we are under great obligations to you both. Tell the children I shall write to them all as I am able, but they must wait for that, but one of them write each week. I hope letters will be on their way before you get this we shall be so anxious.

With much love & many prayers, I am your affectionate
Sister

Emily

Letter #42 – Emily to her children, visiting in America

Birm. Monday Sep 13th 1869

My dear Pollie & Emmie

Another Sunday has passed & we have not yet been to chapel. Yesterday it rained fast all morning, indeed it had done so all the previous night, blowing so furiously that my heart almost failed me many times. I saw you over & over again tossed about on the wide ocean, sick & almost despairing, until I would fancy the very worst, then I had to flee to my refuge, prayer & trust in God, who is able to do all things & who I hope will bring you safe to your destination. I have been at the shop every day but one since you left including Wednesday & Saturday & this is the first day I have had a nap except Sunday. Indeed I have scarcely needed one, as we have gone to bed so early, last night we went to bed at five minutes past nine. We could not sit up any longer, we had read & said all we wanted to & there was no one to amuse us so went to bed. We get up early in a morning, your Pa always goes by the first train.

Stroud returned on Friday night and came up to see me, he staid a little, nursed the baby, listened to the music box & then left as I suppose it was too dull for him. I wish he would not smoke so much, one never sees him without a cigar & I heard from Aunt Radnale that one of the evenings before you went he felt so dull there, that your Aunt Smith fetched some cards downstairs & he played some games with her. There is no fear of your Uncle Smith troubling you, your Aunt had a letter from him thus morning, in which he told her that she must not expect to hear from him again for some time as he was going three or four hundred miles west, it appears your Aunt has never known his address, all her letters have been left at the Post Office, Philadelphia. I think he has given her the slip this time, she is in great trouble about it & talks of getting a situation & putting Johnny into the blue school.

Tuesday 14. Your Pa fetched a Lpool [Liverpool] paper this morning in hope of seeing the arrival of the "Antwerp", but we were disappointed. We wait patiently till tomorrow morning when I shall surely expect to see the much desired news.

I left your Pa to post the letter I wrote to Queenstown & by some misunderstanding he sent nearly all your portraits. The Postmaster did not think it would be in time. We have been expecting to recieve them back again, but conclude as they have not yet turned up, that they must have reached you. You had better send me some back, as I am beset with applicants for them.

Your Grandma is progressing towards recovery, we all thought this time that she must die. She may thank your Pa that she has not, for his untiring zeal in supplying her with everything that would nourish her & do her good.

The baby is much better, her cough has not left her but is less frequent & the paroxysnes [?] are not quite so alarming. Clara's cough is better. It was not Wooping cough with her & I am glad Georgie has not taken it yet, & hope he will not do so.

Give my love to your Aunt Lillie. Tell her I will write to her soon. I owe her a letter of thanks for her handsome present to the baby.

16th. Yesterday our minds were greatly relieved by the news that the "Antwerp" had arrived at New York on Tuesday morning at five o'-clock. I cannot tell you how thankful I felt to see it; it was a great load removed from my mind, & last night when the wind almost blew a hurricane I had no fears, just as though yours had been the only vessel out at sea, & your lives the only ones at stake. I long to hear about your voyage & everything connected with it.

Yesterday Stroud came in with his pictures, at least two of them he has just had taken at Oldham & Cookers [?], but they were not good. I told him I would not send one of those, so he went back & had them taken again.

We have an opposition [?] "bus" as far as Bloomsburg, & now ride all the way for twopence.

It is George Elallily's [?] birth-day & I am going there to tea. Your Pa is to be there when he has closed the shop, & Rachael is to be at home. I am taking her a book as you promised, Ministoring Children [?] and George for a birthday present Gullivers Travels.

I cannot stay to say more as I expect George to call for me in a few minutes, & I want this mailed tonight.

With much love to you all & many prayers that God may bless you
I am your loving
Mother

E. Cadby

Tell Aunt Lewis I intended to have written her with this but must do so next time.

Tell your Grandma, she must write me a long letter.

Letter #43 – Sister-in-law Amanda to Emily

Amanda writes a letter to Emily, giving updates on Emily's children, with the kind of specific details she understands Emily would want to have. Emily and her three visiting children would never see each other again.

Troy, N.Y. Nov. 7th [1869]

My Dear Sister Emily:

It is not my usual habit to do any letter writing on Sunday, but this afternoon, as I was sitting alone I thought I should enjoy a little chat with you so ink and paper must carry my thoughts to you.

The children have probably written you what confusion we have been in ever since our return. Part of the time we have not had a clean chair to sit on, and we have had no servant girl. For the last week we have taken our meals at Ma's but before that George made the fires in the morning and Emmie and I got the meals. She has assisted me greatly, has done all the marketing and running of errands. Three or four times she has cooked the dinner herself; roasting meat, cooking vegetables and making pies. She is a capital girl, possessing every quality that I admire. I only wonder how you ever spared her. Nothing but a preemptory order from yourself for her return would induce me to part with her. My acquaintance with her has been short, but it has ripened into a love which could scarcely be stronger if she were my own child. George is very fond of her and I think she is of him and feels his displeasure. We are anxious to do every thing for her pleasure and improvement. I have decided it will be best to teach her at home and she is pleased with the idea. She will have two hours of study per day and I shall hear her recite, then three hours of piano practice will occupy her time fully. We are all settled now and she will begin immediately. We have fitted up a little room next to ours and bought her a very pretty set of Chestnut furniture. I shall try to teach her to keep it in perfect order. I have shortened her green reps [?] and finished her plaid. The Winsey has been washed and I had that to make over and let out. I think she has grown an inch or more, she is ever so much taller than Polly. I shall make her some cotton flannel drawers, and have her wear thick stockings, she seems to feel the cold very much. She is a bright, obedient, kind girl and if she writes that she is contented you may rest, satisfied that all is right. She received your letter a few days since and will answer soon. She has quite a disagreeable cold in her head just now, but she will be better soon, I hope.

Last week we had a very pleasant family gathering at Alfred's on the occasion of Lillie's birthday and I presume we shall celebrate Thanksgiving Day, George's and Emmie's birthdays on the 18th of this month at our house. Edmund is still at Albany and wants a family party in his rooms this week. He is very attentive to a young lady there and we surmise that it means something serious. His health is very poor and I wish he had an affectionate strong wife to take care of him. We were very glad he did not go to the West Indies. Ma has a cold which kept her in bed one day, but it is remarkable how well she is. She attends to her household duties, as though she were well. We are astonished to see Aunt Lewis about again. She walked over to our house yesterday, with Polly's assistance. We never expected to see her out of her room again. Polly has been very attentive to her and waited on her almost entirely during her illness. She is also becoming quite a seamstress under Mary's instructions. She mends all the stockings and she showed me a very nice piece of darning she had done on her merino dress. She is making herself a night dress and yesterday she was shortening her green dress. She has become quite disgusted with long dresses, and will not have anything but short dresses. She is looking very well and seems very happy. I saw her as she started to Sunday School this afternoon. She wore her new plaid suit, ermine furs and Paris hat. Not many girls are prettier than she when dressed becomingly.

I want to tell you most of John for I know you felt most anxious about him. I want to tell you the plain truth without any flowering and my simple opinion of him. I feel convinced that he has greatly improved in appearance, behavior and in thought, and that he will be a help to his Uncle and become a success as a business man. He must have gained several pounds in flesh, and his face looks flush and full. He is ready for three good, solid meals per day and does justice to them. He seems much more polite and thoughtful of others wants. He takes the boys' jokes very kindly, never exhibiting anger over them but evidently profiting by their hints. He is very much interested in church and Sunday School, the choir, prayer meetings and church societies, attending them all very regularly. He never spends an evening out without some of the family with him. George has lent him his organ and he practices on it a good deal. Alfred has also bought him a violin and is giving him lessons. I think he has given up all desire for low company and seeks to improve himself. He is very steady at the store from morning until night but seems quite satisfied with it. He keeps himself looking very tidy and is always ready to talk and make himself agreeable. A few evenings since, as we all sat at tea, someone asked John if he had heard you had been very ill, he looked amazed and said No, is there another baby? We all laughed and had a joke at his expense.

It is scarcely appropriate for me to extend my sympathy to you for your mishap, knowing as I do, that you were very glad. I only hope that such a thing may not occur again and that you may soon regain your accustomed strength. I dreamed of John, a few nights ago, and when I wakened I could scarcely believe I was not in your house and had been talking to him. Indeed I wish we could gather round your hearth again and spend a pleasant evening together as we used. I shall ever feel indebted to John until he comes and visits us. I can assure him a most hearty welcome from every member of the family and the hospitalities of six families await him. Can you not persuade him to come before many months more have passed? We have the small picture he gave us, framed and hanging in the parlor, the large one is at the shop being framed, we have saved a space for it over the piano. The "sleeping children" are kept on the marble slab in front of the mirror. Everyone admires them so much. Mr and Mrs Francis returned from their European trip last week. Mary took Polly to call on them. They brought a great many beautiful things. Mr and Mrs Crocker have also returned. They speak very highly of you to Edmund.

We have had most delightful weather for the past week it being our "Indian Summer". Today it has snowed and the wind blows as though winter had really set in. Stoves are all up and we are glad to hover over and around them. George is not as well as I could wish. He is so anxious about every thing that it wears upon his brain. I hope, someday, he may leave business and join John in buying a farm. I have a severe cold, but otherwise I am perfectly well. I am bustling about all day, and when we have a girl I shall have my hands more than full of serving. I am afraid Emmie will never accomplish much with her needle. She will be most efficient on the piano and in her singing. Mary's health is better but I am afraid she will never be strong and well. She and Joseph are most interested in the children, invite them to tea very frequently and take them about to see different objects of interest. Fred and Fannie agree about as well as usual, she will never be any better. He leads a wretched life. Freddie is a bright, interesting little boy.

I am interested to know when you are going to be able to spare Flora for me. I liked her very much and will be ready for her whenever you can ship her. I suppose she is your woman now, being the oldest daughter at home. I have written much more than I have intended. I hope part of it will prove interesting at least. We are always glad to receive your letters and would not object to reading one occasionally from John. Please give our love to him. George will write at his first leisure, he has been very busy with the house improvements. I will write again when opportunity presents itself.

From your affectionate sister,

Amanda

The Cluett Cadby correspondence ends here.

Emily Cluett Cadby died the following year at age forty, after giving birth to her eleventh child, October 10, 1870. The baby, named Amanda, died as well.

After Emily's death, John Cadby emigrated to America with his seven remaining children, joining the three children already in America who were staying with members of the Cluett family in Troy.

John Cadby settled in Hudson, New York. It is unclear whether he worked in either of the Cluett businesses (music, or collar making). Daughter Emmie (Emily) continued to live in Troy with George and Amanda Cluett; Polly (Mary), who had been living with her grandparents, joined her father John to help take care of the family.

John Cadby (Sr.), along with Emily, is buried in the Cluett family plot in Oakwood Cemetery, Troy, N.Y.

Debt, Faith and Fortune

A View of William Cluett And His Debt

The Cluett Cadby letters detail the early years for my Cluett ancestors in Troy, N.Y., when my grandfather's grandfather Robert was a child. For me the letters are fresh and familiar: their love of words and music, their strong feeling for each other, and their compelling faith, leap off the page and I feel as though I could walk into a room and be at home with this line of my ancestors.

Having failed in business and fleeing debt, the family had much both to lament and to be thankful for. The letters are infused with expressions of their Christian faith and of their feeling for each other, the eight who emigrated and the one left behind. The yearnings to see each other concur with a wish expressed to fulfill God's will.

Reading these letters prompted me to ask questions about what the legacy of the Cluetts' accomplishments and their wealth was for the following generations, but also what was the legacy of their faith in Christianity? I found questions about their faith kept circling back to the 'elephant in the room' — the debt that the Cluetts fled and that they had such mixed feelings about.

What follows is a consideration of the role that debt and faith played in that family, with a look at the reverberations from those outlooks that I feel so many generations later.

The lens I look through is both celebratory and critical. While I admire what the Cluetts accomplished, I notice the efforts to conceal what they left behind; while I feel their intimate family pull and the grief of being apart, I also see pressure and manipulation, particularly by the mother, Ann. I notice family rifts (however brief, between John Cadby and his brother-in-law, Reverend Joseph Mulford); black sheep (John Cadby Jr., who after moving to America begins to move away from associating with 'low company'); and relationships that other family members wonder at ('Fred and Fannie got along about as usual').

All of this richness of human experience fascinates me, and yet I keep coming back to what stands out for me in the letters and related documents — the extraordinary perceived righteousness of William and his offspring, as set against the efforts on the part of the family to hide what brought them to Troy in the first place.

We discover in the opening letter that the central decision in William's life, leading to his family's phenomenal prosperity and ascent in America, was to flee the many debts that he had accrued in England. This fact, while known by his immediate family, was one that he worked during his life to keep a secret from his community in Troy.

Ann repeatedly counsels her children to be faithful to God and turn their thoughts to Him; at the same time she fears no retribution for their decision to abandon their financial commitments to others in England. Through the letters Ann communicates the view that, effectively, now on the other side of the ocean, there's nothing their creditors can do, and their faith in God will absolve them of guilt "*for* [we] *had no choice*".

The debts are referred to numerous times in the letters, but the completion of repayment of them for William is almost always in the future, or when "*gold is down*". In later years, Ann speaks of paying off the debts herself from her "*housekeeping money*", that she has "*out at interest*". However, although she is earning interest herself, the overdue debts would be repaid "*without interest*". Subsequently we see in the letters (#29, #32 and #33) that neither she nor William takes immediate action to follow through on their stated intentions.

Seventeen years after migrating the Cluetts continued to put off repayment of the debts. By that time they were well off, and central figures in the churches of Troy. One of their friends (who three years earlier is described as the first who will be repaid) dies without ever being repaid, despite gold prices having come down substantially. After his death, Ann says, "*I will send his widow the money,*" but we do not know whether that debt, or the others of lower priority, were ever repaid.

William's obituary (Appendix F) underlines his business and family accomplishments but more particularly his moral standing in the community. He is described as bringing with him to America, "*above all...* [a] *character of inflexible uprightness*", an impression of character that William worked hard in America to establish, while burying his past.

In reading the Cluett Cadby letters I have been struck by two qualities of William Cluett's family. I have found the vitality of their Christian faith to be moving and infectious: they met uncertainty and loss with a resolute and ever-renewing confidence in God's guiding hand. While building their own families and lives they were constantly looking to help others, and to in active and practical ways support communities and institutions that they believed would serve the wider good. I see their faith as a living presence that fed and sustained their daily lives.

But the other attribute I see in the letters is the concern of the Cluetts to maintain an appearance of righteousness, by hiding or covering the parts of themselves or their actions that would be considered less than ideal. While this behaviour may be natural in human functioning, my sense is that in the Cluett family, and in their descendants, the need to appear 'better than' was very pronounced, and was related to their spiritual - and material - ambitions. This heightened awareness of, and the guarding of, an appearance of righteousness is very familiar to me.

In William's family there was a clear overlap between a concern about their appearance of righteousness, and the choice to be dishonest, with its inevitable corollary, self-deception. The concern to appear righteous is certainly not unique to the Cluett family.

William and Ann's great-grandsons, John Parmenter Cluett and Gorham Cluett, grandchildren of shirt manufacturer and philanthropist George B. Cluett, retained the family need to establish a flawless family reputation. Their views, both of William and of the threat of moral stain left by his flight from debt, are clear in their preamble to a set of eight Cluett letters they had in their possession, along with newspaper clippings about the Cluetts' accomplishments, which they copied for their families in 1967:

> *As to any debts that William Cluett left unpaid in England, a full reading of this volume* [the eight letters and clippings] *will convince*

the most skeptical that it is simply inconceivable that in view of the tremendous moral, religious and financial responsibility of this entire family that any money owed to anyone here or abroad was not eventually paid in full. [See Appendix E.]

Then, in 1982, Virginia Horger Grogan (Emily's great-granddaughter), in introducing a larger set of the letters in a family newsletter, remarked similarly on the connection between William's debts and his moral stature:

> *Because of references in old letters to William's having left England in rather a hurry and with debts to be paid, one might get the idea that he was not an honorable man. Nothing could be further from the truth. The debts were paid and the future conduct of his life is proof that he was a man of principle in all his dealings.**

William and Ann's granddaughter Emmie Cadby recalled the financial strain that her parents were under in England in the earliest years after William's flight (see Appendix D). Her parents, Emily and her new husband John Cadby in England, had to face creditors and also their shocked business and social peers. They were obliged to repay as many of William's debts as they could in order to carry on in business themselves.

The divide between William's act in England, and his efforts to establish a reputation in America as wholly honest, was a wide one. The burying of truth in order to be seen as surpassingly ideal has an effect: William set up a split within himself, guarding his view of himself as a conscientious and moral Christian, one who was fit to preach and lead by example in America, at the same time that he was avoiding repaying his creditors in England.

The remarks of William's descendants affirm their belief that William paid off his debts. While defending William, his descendants seem to suggest that because William paid off his debts he was a righteous man. The implication is that, while William may have run off on debts, his repayment of them 'rights the wrong'. The descendants, as inheritors of that righteousness, vigorously assert this repayment.

* Virginia Horger Grogan and Emily Rodemann, "Dorlon-Moore-Cluett Cadby – How their descendants found happiness in Rensselaer County", from the family newsletters, 1981-1985.

However William himself seemed to know that repaying the debts he fled would never wholly right the wrong — he knew that he had broken faith, and stolen money from his lenders — to some perhaps never repaying it, and to others, repaying when he wanted but certainly not under the terms in which the loan was understood initially (that is, many years later, and without interest).

I believe his avoidance of repayment was not just a reluctance to part with the money (which I also think it was), but more importantly I see in his avoidance a reluctance to face what he had done, by having any contact with those he had harmed, even if repaying a debt many years later. Their view of him would remain compromised even if they were eventually recompensed.

It is an example of how we cultivate a divide in the ways we see ourselves: we turn a blind eye to parts of our lives, while working to reinforce our self-image in other areas, seeking the approval of others to confirm the image we want of ourselves.

The idea that a person is either entirely honorable — or not at all — is enhanced by the act of Christian idealization. There is a damaging effect in the notion that an individual is either wholly ideal, or wholly stained. A common occurrence in families who seek to see themselves as ideal is the 'black sheep', the member who must bear the brunt of family flaws, as they carry the shame for the group.

I see a degree of spiritual and relational challenge down through the Cluett family. Intra-familial rifts or relationship breakdown often have as their root a moral principle: stand-offs occur as each party sees itself as holding the higher moral ground. Shame as a compounding element feeds the rifts, the exclusions, and the sense of either being morally justified, or, on the other side, 'despised and rejected'.

These tendencies occur in all families, but I suspect that in ambitious families — and the Cluetts were ambitious in worldly matters, and in spiritual matters — the rifts, the passionate disagreements and the breakdowns may be even more pronounced.

The aspiration to righteousness (coupled with a tendency to bury attributes that do not meet the good image we have of ourselves) can feed the conviction of our own freedom from fault, while supporting the distancing of ourselves from those we see as falling short of our ideals.

To some extent such polarizing can be laid at the feet of a practice of Christianity that focuses on the contrast between those who are righteous, and those who are not. I see this righteous polarizing happening in our culture, and not just in Christian circles but in the broader secular world, where any group or individual holding a passionate belief that their cause has a high moral value can easily slip into vilifying those who hold the other point of view.

Polarization, so often rooted in what each side believes to be a 'right' cause, increases conflict and renders compromise more difficult. The poles move further apart the more entrenched each side is, and the more each side digs in on their convictions.

That wish on the part of William Cluett's family to be seen as righteous was one that was familiar to me, and it is a wish I have come to question in my own life. From a young age, and without being particularly aware of it, I wanted to be good — and to be seen as good. It is for this reason in part that William's family struck me as so astonishingly familiar. But inevitably a focus on goodness also includes identifying what (or who) is bad. I have found that the outcome is not a healthy and diverse whole, made up of imperfect human beings, but rather may be a fractured entity (relationship, family, or institution) that experiences an increase in conflict and polarization.

These traits of the Cluetts strike me as familiar, in part because I come from that family, but cultural and religious links connect me to so many beyond the family group. It is these two lines of Christian experience that I am working to parse out — a vital faith, as set against an identification with righteousness that is groomed societally, and institutionally through the church and other institutions both religious and secular. Can one build on the former (a vital and evolving faith), while relinquishing the latter (the polarizing effects of the grooming of righteousness)?

For some years I have, along with others in Two Fishes Press, been reflecting on the Christian faith. The fundamental moral disjuncture that I see in my ancestral family, a family that was so focused on righteousness, tells me something about why I began questioning the focus on righteousness for myself, even before reading the letters.

I see a connection with the Christian faith being probed in my parents' generation and in mine, largely through examining and challenging the bounds of what had been set before us in Christian culture, its institutions and its texts. My own search for a vital link with Christianity has included working against basic (and learned) tendencies to polarize: that tendency to want to see ourselves as good and others as not.

What stays with me after this immersion in the letters and lives of William Cluett and his family are their humanity and their flaws, their humour and their powerful desire to overcome obstacles in order to stay together. However, the complicated thread of Christianity that runs through Cluett family history, and is so much a part of my cultural and familial make-up, leaves me continuing to ask what in Christianity needs redeeming now.

DEBT IN VICTORIAN ENGLAND

Debtors' prisons were common in England up until the mid-19th Century. Meant alternately as holding grounds or places of punishment for those who could not pay their debts, the prisons gained a horrific reputation.

Attitudes and laws around debt and insolvency were going through a transition at the time of William Cluett's departure for America in 1850. Imprisonment for debt was increasingly seen as inhumane, and also not very effective for ensuring that debts got repaid. In the decade before William emigrated, three of London's largest debtors prisons were closed down (Fleet, 1842; Marshalsea, 1842; and Faringdon, 1846). By 1869, imprisonment for debt was reserved for particular circumstances, where either fraud or malice of intention was proven.

As a business owner William Cluett was a member of the rising middle class in Victorian England. He had a place in society and some privileges where debt was concerned, not available to the working class at that time. It is far more likely that William would have faced bankruptcy than a term in prison, and his creditors would have initiated the process of declaring William bankrupt. By 1849 William would also have had the option of taking some control of his finances by personally declaring bankruptcy (while those with non-trade or personal debt became 'insolvent debtors' and could not declare bankruptcy).

While imprisonment for debt was becoming less common by 1850, it was still possible to be jailed for debt through 1869. Fundamentally such imprisonment affected the lower classes, who either did not meet the criteria for declaring bankruptcy, or who lacked the means to get financial help from friends or family.

Declaring bankruptcy (or having it declared for you by your creditors) might have spared William from debtors' prison. However bankruptcy brought with it not just the confiscation of all assets and belongings but the removal of financial autonomy, and perhaps more importantly the loss of reputation and standing in society, as bankruptcies were publicized in order to serve as a deterrent for others.

In the Victorian era bankruptcy was a criminal offence, and with it came disgrace for the debtor's family and even their social circle. The prospect of the social and personal devastation consequent upon having bankruptcy declared for you by your creditors, or in choosing to declare bankruptcy yourself, would have been terrifying.

SOURCES

https://www.legislation.gov.uk/ukpga/1869/62/pdfs/ukpga_18690062_en.pdf

http://victorian-era.org/debt-prisons-of-victorian-era-england.html

http://victorian-era.org/victorian-era-economy.html

https://valmcbeath.com/victorian-era-middle-classes/

https://valmcbeath.com/victorian-era-bankruptcy/

Faith – The Cluetts and the Church

William Cluett, before migrating to America, lived in the town of Wolverhampton, in Staffordshire, England. He was active in the Methodist church, and often took the post of lay traveling preacher, a key role in the structure of Methodism. Within a year of arriving in Troy, William was eager to take up the role of traveling preacher again with the Methodist church there, and he soon had congregations to whom he preached. (His awareness of moral conflict over this is evident in the letters!)

It is clear from references in the letters that William prioritized the building of his theological library, while his eagerness for church news from England

Pastor, Trustees, and Stewards of State Street Church, 1874.
Robert Cluett is seated, 2nd from left. J.W.A. Cluett is standing, 4th from left. Edmund Cluett is standing, 5th from left. George B. Cluett is standing, 6th from left. [From *The History of Methodism in Troy N.Y.*, by Joseph Hillman, Troy, 1888.]

and a number of theological texts he left behind is expressed. William was a well-read and fundamentally well-educated man, albeit neither in college nor in a seminary.

We hear in the letters that Ann makes her first appearance 'in society' in Troy by beginning again to attend church, and soon Mary and her brothers are participating in Sunday school. Mary writes of a religious revival in Troy (in letter #17), and in letter #12 she discusses how her young brothers meet on their own weekly with other boys doing a prayer meeting. (This is difficult to picture in the 21st century!)

Music was an important aspect of worship; Mary worked as a music teacher, and Frederick for years was an organist in the churches of Troy. Each of the children played an instrument and sang, and they were often invited to perform for others.

In adulthood we see (in *The History of Methodism in Troy, N.Y.*) that each of the five Cluett sons held leadership positions in State Street Church, the Methodist

Official Board of State Street Church, 1887-88.
Rev. William Cluett is standing, far left. Frederick Cluett is seated, far right.
[From *The History of Methodism in Troy N.Y.*, by Joseph Hillman, Troy, 1888.]

Episcopal church in Troy, where William became deacon Reverend Cluett. However the Cluetts were also active in and donated to other churches in Troy.

During her married life, Mary Cluett Mulford and her husband Reverend Joseph Mulford, along with Mary's nephew Sanford Cluett, helped to found an early Episcopal church in Florida — Bethesda-By-The-Sea at Palm Beach, still extant today (and still displaying the early pews made from the slats of liquor crates!) The Cluett garden there is now a tourist attraction.

New State Street M.E. Church, Troy, constructed 1871.
This is the Methodist Episcopal church that the Cluetts attended. This replaced the original church built in 1827.
[From *The History of Methodism in Troy N.Y.*, by Joseph Hillman, Troy, 1888.]

The practice of Christianity was central in the life of the Cluett family, beginning before their migration in 1850, and well into the twentieth century. Eldest son Albert (J.W.A.) published a hymnal, and youngest son Robert published three books for aiding in Christian worship or devotions.

The book, *Day By Day With The Master: Scripture Readings with Prayers for Use of Young People*, was published by Robert Cluett, Sr., in 1920. In that family line, almost-daily prayer for the extended family was still practiced until Robert's daughter-in-law, Amy Knight Cluett, began to resist the pressure to family piety, and withdrew her own family from such gatherings in the late 1920's or early 1930's.

Fortune – Cluett & Sons Music

Cluett & Sons was founded by William Cluett in 1854, first as a book and sheet-music store, and then built up as a music store in cooperation with his sons, Edmund and Frederick, expanding over the following fifty years. In its heyday, it primarily sold musical instruments, specializing in pianos and related instruments (player pianos, organs, etc.). Eventually Cluett & Sons also sold radios and televisions.

In the Hart Cluett Museum is a 1902 store catalogue, printed by Frederick H. Cluett, twelve years after William had died and in the period when William's sons Frederick and Edmund ran the business along with Fred's son, Frederick Jr., and others. By 1902 Cluett & Sons had eleven branch stores across three states.

In order to celebrate the opening of a large new Cluett & Sons music store in Troy in 1902, an illustrated catalogue was printed. Of particular interest is Fred's account in that catalogue of William's migration to America, with careful wording about why William emigrated, and (naturally) no mention of his sudden flight from debt: *"Being solicitous of the welfare of this family, and having several sons, he felt that there would be more advantages for them in the United States; and therefore, after due consideration, sailed for America in the month of June, 1850…."*

Cluett & Sons – Pianos, Organs, Musical Merchandise and Sheet Music

> We take great pleasure and quite a little pride in presenting this souvenir [catalogue], with its illustrations of our new quarters, to our patrons and friends. Commercial history relates many tales of the modest beginnings of some of our greatest enterprises, and not a few are told of the piano industry; therefore, without the least desire to dim the success of others, we

merely express a few facts relating to our entrance and early efforts in the piano trade.

William Cluett, the founder of this house, was born in the village of Hilton Staffordshire [actually in neighbouring county Shropshire], England, in 1806. He was known as a book connoisseur and widely read man, and was engaged for many years in the book business having stores in Birmingham and London. Being solicitous of the welfare of this family, and having several sons, he felt that there would be more advantages for them in the United States; and therefore, after due consideration, sailed for America in the month of June, 1850, making the journey to New York in a sailing vessel, the voyage lasting more than six weeks. He landed at Troy on the steamboat "Empire," on July 18th.

In November, 1854, he opened a book and piano store at No. 75 Congress Street. The main floor was used for the book department; the upper story for the sale and exhibition of the Grovesteen & Truslow pianos. Finding these quarters too small, it was decided in 1856 to enlarge, and a store was secured at No. 266 River Street. As the business increased rapidly, it was soon found necessary to secure more room, and additional space was obtained in the adjoining stores.

In the following year, William Cluett's eldest son, J.W.A. Cluett, became associated with him, and the firm took the name of "William Cluett & Son." In 1863, J.W.A. Cluett withdrew from the firm to engage in the manufacture of collars and cuffs, and became associated with the house of George B. Cluett, Brother and Co. In the same year, two other sons, Edmund and Fred. H. Cluett, became partners of their father, and the firm name was changed to "Cluett & Sons."

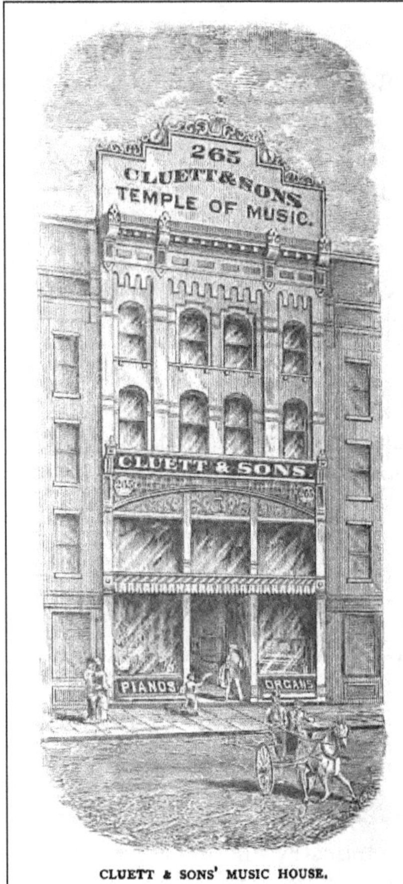

Cluett & Sons music store, Troy, New York. 1886
[From *The City of Troy and Its Vicinity*, by Arthur James Weiss, Troy, 1886]

This change added new vigor and enthusiasm to those interested, and the business increased so rapidly that their present location was found to be inadequate, and in 1865 they moved to No. 261 River Street. Here indeed were spacious quarters when compared with those recently occupied. The book business was given up, and a sheet music and musical merchandise department was introduced, making this house a thoroughly equipped and up-to-date music establishment.

The honorable reputation of this house was becoming widely known, and in 1868, a branch store was opened in Albany, in the Delevan House Block. In 1871, another change in location was made, the firm moving to No. 265 River Street. The business increased rapidly, not only in the adjacent territory, but extending into the adjoining states of Vermont and Massachusetts. In order to better cover the territory, branch warerooms were opened in various places, until at the present time (1902) the firm is operating stores in Troy, Albany, Schenectady, Gloversville, Oneonta, Glens Falls, Plattsburgh, N.Y.; Bennington, Burlington, and Rutland, Vt.; and North Adams, Mass.

In the early 80's, Fred. H. Cluett's eldest son, Charles Fred., and W. Irving Johnson, started their apprenticeships in the sheet music department, and as boys together, sparing neither brain nor energy, their devotion to the interests of the firm knew no limit, and as experience developed, they became thoroughly conversant with the details of the business, The appreciation of their services was well demonstrated by their admission into the firm in January, 1901.

Progressiveness has always been a characteristic of this house, and it was thought best to secure a building especially fitted to meet the requirements of modern methods of conducting a first-class piano establishment. After months of preparation, all was in readiness, and between the hours of six o-clock in the evening of April 30th, and eight o'clock in the morning of May 1st, 1902, the almost unprecedented feat was performed of moving a house of this magnitude to its present location; the extend of which some little idea may be gained from the following descriptive and photographic reproductions.

The catalogue has page after page of photographs of the showroom floors of their music business, largely selling pianos. The "New location" was likely The Cannon Block, Troy, N.Y..

Fortune – Cuffs, Collars and Shirts

The cuff and collar business that George B. Cluett entered as a young man (Maullin and Blanchard, c. 1854) later become Cluett, Brothers & Co., and over the decades merged with other cuff and collar companies — first Coon & Co., and later Peabody and Co. The longest running iteration of the Cluett cuff, collar and shirt business was Cluett, Peabody & Co., which grew to become the largest shirt manufacturer in the world in the first half of the twentieth century.

In addition to brothers George B. Cluett, J.W. Alfred and Robert, other Cluetts worked in the company. The sons of George and Robert were employed in the company and had leadership roles, and nephews came in as well.

Cluett, Peabody & Co. Collar, Cuff and Shirt Factory, Troy, N.Y., c.1910.
[The Valentine-Souvenir Co., New York.]

Sanford Cluett (son of brother Edmund) joined the factory and began to tinker to improve production. Sanford's best-known invention was a process called 'Sanforizing', invented in 1928 and still in use today, which limited shrinkage of the finished shirts.

In its heyday Cluett, Peabody & Co. had factories internationally and produced millions of shirts annually. Most famous was their product, the Arrow shirt (and its marketing mascot, The Arrow Man). The plants in the Troy area were divided between the Bleachery on Peebles Island, where the shirt textiles were prepared, and the sprawling Cluett & Peabody factory buildings in downtown Troy where the cuffs, collars and shirts were cut and assembled.

Troy still carries the nickname 'The Collar City'. A number of cuff, collar and shirt companies were established in Troy in the mid-nineteenth century, when such companies proliferated after sewing machines began to be used in manufacturing. However, the largest of these was Cluett, Peabody and Co., which continued internationally with its well-known "Monarch" and "Arrow" shirt brands until it was taken over by Westpoint Pepperell in the late 1980's.

SOURCES

A.J Weise, *History of the City of Troy*. Troy: William H. Young, 1876
https://archive.org/details/citytroyanditsv00weisgoog/page/n96/mode/2up?q=Cluett&view=theater - online archive of A.J. Weise's, 'History of the City of Troy'

https://hoxsie.org/2012/02/07/cluett_peabody_co/ - Nice summary of Cluett, Peabody and Co.

https://www.hmdb.org/m.asp?m=115364 - Historical marker, 'What Happened At The Bleachery?'

http://14to42.net/19streetw022.html - Cluett, Peabody & Co. in New York City

https://hoxsie.org/2012/02/06/how_the_collar_city_got_its_name/

https://en.wikipedia.org/wiki/Cluett_Peabody_%26_Company

Epilogue

Letters, Genealogies and Encounters

After Emily died, we have no more access to the lives of William Cluett and his offspring through their (known) letters. The Cluetts' rise in business and their impressive success were evident not only in the size of their companies, but in their property holdings, with fine summer homes in Saratoga, New York; Palm Beach, Florida, and Williamstown, Massachusetts, as well as dwellings in the wealthier neighbourhoods of Troy in the late nineteenth and early twentieth century. The "Marble House" at the Hart Cluett Museum is one Cluett home in Troy still standing from that era. George B. and Robert Cluett, in the shirt, cuff and collar business, left substantial estates for their heirs[1]. Summaries of the individual histories of William's children can be found online, and through Ginny Grogan's research that appears in Appendix B.

While the public and business lives of the Cluetts are well documented, we hear little of life in the home, outside of letters (such as we have here), or journals (such as that left by George B. Cluett's wife, Amanda Rockwell Cluett).

In contemplating the arc of life, particularly for the Cluett women, I was struck with the wide variation in the survival rate of their children. (See Appendix A for a list of the children and grandchildren of William and Ann Cluett.) Many individuals living in the second half of the nineteenth century faced the now rare (for North Americans) and devastating loss of a child.

Of all of William's children, eldest son Alfred (J.W.A.) and his wife Lillie were most tragically affected by infant mortality. Of their seven children, only two reached adulthood. Two daughters survived; one married but had no children; the other married and had one daughter, who had no children. There are no J.W.A. Cluett descendants.

Given that the Cluetts lived in a city with hospitals and doctors, and were well off, the fact that they were little protected against infant mortality is a mark of the precariousness of early life in that era. Five of seven children in Alfred's family died, not at birth (a common cause of both infant and maternal mortality at that time), but between the ages of one and six, with four of the five dying between their first and third years. Interestingly, it appears that none of Emily's children died in infancy in England, except her eleventh child who died, as did mother Emily, from complications of the birth.

George B. Cluett lost his first wife, Sarah Golden (and child), to death in childbirth, in an apparent case of eclampsia (described in detail in letter #31, in 1864), and then he and his second wife, Amanda Rockwell Fisher, also lost their firstborn in infancy. He and Amanda lost a second child, Bessie, three years later, at less than a year old, and another, Alfonzo, in young adulthood. In Amanda's journal of 1900-1917, she speaks frequently of grieving first the loss of Alfonzo, and then her husband George.

Fannie and Fred also lost two children in infancy; Fannie had a child in 1866, and then lost a baby in 1868; she lost another in 1869; and then gave birth to another baby (who survived) in 1870. (On a side note — in the letters, Fannie is often described as being disagreeable, initially in 1868, and again in 1869; in the second instance more extremely so. By 1869, when the second letter was written, Fannie had been pregnant for three of the preceding four years, and may have, by this date, lost two babies in a row. In less than five years Fannie was pregnant with and gave birth to four babies, two of whom died in infancy. Perhaps some of her disagreeability was related to this situation?)

A look at the survival rate of the Cluett grandchildren gives a glimpse into life on the home front, as does a rare surviving note from 1873, written by one of the Cluett sisters-in-law, to another, concerning their children.

This handwritten note was a reply to a birthday invitation, written by J.W. Alfred Cluett's wife, Lillie Bontecou Cluett, to her sister-in-law, Amanda Cluett (wife of George B. Cluett), answering in the affirmative for the 3rd Birthday Party of Walter Herbert Cluett (George and Amanda's eldest, after their first child died in infancy).

Four children are named in the note: Percy Cadby, aged 9 (apparently staying with Alfred and Lillie after the migration of widowed John Cadby and his children); Jessie Cluett (Alfred and Lillie's first daughter, here aged six); Minnie Cluett (Alfred and Lillie's second daughter, Jessie's twin, also six); and their son Stanley Cluett (aged two). The note says:

> *Misses Jessie and Minnie Cluett and Masters Percy Cadby and Stanley Cluett accept with much pleasure Master Walter Herbert Cluett's invitation for Wednesday next and hope to be able to play, but most especially to "eat", a great deal, between the hours of 2 and 6 p.m. Feb. 24th 1873.*

At the time of this party, Alfred and Lillie had already lost two children in infancy. In the year following this birthday party, two more of their children, who are named in the note — Minnie at age six, and Stanley at age two — also died. That two of the children at this party (here eating, playing, and celebrating a birthday with the other children) died so soon afterwards brings home the heartbreak of those early deaths.

With respect to early mortality, my great-aunt Marjorie Cluett (Duane) died at age twenty-three in the Influenza Pandemic in 1919. Marjorie was my grandfather Robert III's only sibling. In addition to being given Marjorie's name, I was given her early sketchbooks and writing when I was a child. Her death, forty-two years before my birth, seemed close and real to me; being given her name and the tangible remnants from her young life helped kindle my interest in the lives of those earlier family members.

Marjorie's first cousin Emily, daughter of Robert Jr.'s brother George Alfred (Al), also died in the Influenza Pandemic at age eighteen. Thus Robert Cluett (Sr.), as privileged as he was, lost two of his grandchildren in young adulthood in the early twentieth century, before the young women had children themselves.

In my father's Cluett-family archive, there are two extensive written genealogies, which attempt to trace lineage prior to William Cluett: one handwritten, possibly within a decade of William's death in 1890, and the other, hardbound, that was commissioned during the 1940's by two of William's grandchildren, Robert Cluett Jr. ('Bert') and Sanford Lockwood Cluett, and completed by an esteemed professional genealogist. In their 1964 preamble to a smaller group of these letters which they copied for their families, John and Gorham Cluett (see Appendix E) refer to a genealogy. That genealogy was likely the one which was commissioned in the 1930's by Bert and Sanford (first cousins of John and Gorham's father, E. Harold Cluett).

Bert and Sanford were children of William's sons, Robert and Edmund Cluett, and together they did a lot of genealogical research, corresponding about their finds.[2] Eventually they hired a genealogist who traveled to England to work on a family tree, which was bound in book form and distributed in the family.

However, through a close reading of the letters we can see that, prior to William's father's generation, both of the genealogies are entirely wrong.

Robert Cluett, Sr. b.1844
Photo: Shroder studio, Troy, N.Y.
[Robert Cluett IV collection]

Robert Cluett, Jr. b.1869
Photo: Magill studio, Troy, N.Y.
[Robert Cluett IV collection]

Without living individuals to consult, it can be difficult for any family researcher or genealogist who is dependent solely on parish records and other archives to trace family lines, especially those that have many repeated first and last names and similar dates of birth. The genealogy commissioned in the 1930's is only reliable back to William's parents, as we discover in letter #23 (from 1858) when William meets his aunt in Philadelphia. In that conversation (relayed in the letter) we learn that William's father (William Sr.) was the 'only brother' of Elizabeth Newton, the aunt that William (Jr.) meets.

This account of a conversation between living individuals overrides what is shown in the genealogy that was done seventy-five years later, and which showed William Sr. as one of several brothers, at least two of whom lived to adulthood and marriage, with Elizabeth in a different branch of the family (which she was not). We also learn in the 1858 letter (#23) that Elizabeth and William Sr.'s father's name was not Thomas (as indicated in the genealogy), but John.

In the 1930's correspondence between Bert and Sanford, they describe the difficulties in tracing the family tree, and perhaps the reputed genealogist did what he could while researching in England, with all the multiple William, John,

Robert Cluett III. b.1898
Oil on canvas. Artur Lajos Halmi, 1930.
[Author's collection]

Robert Cluett IV. b.1932
Photographer unknown.
[Robert Cluett IV collection]

and Thomas Cluetts who had lived in the Lydlinch area over the centuries, coupled with gaps in birth, baptismal and marriage records. At the very least, this discrepancy shows the difficulty of tracing with accuracy our family trees.

Interestingly, during the 1930's, Sanford Cluett visited the east coast of Canada, where a number of Cluetts resided, looking for distant cousins. Upon making the acquaintance of some Cluetts in Cape Breton (descendants of the Cluett branch that established fisheries in Newfoundland), that cousin was so taken with Sanford that he named his son after him. Coincidentally, that son, Jack Sanford Cluett (born in Nova Scotia in 1934) and Robert Cluett IV (born in New York in 1932) now both live in Prince Edward County, Ontario,where they (distant cousins) have become friends (2022). That Jack, a distant Cluett cousin, and my father Robert, who knew and was more closely related to Sanford Cluett, ended up living in the same community in Ontario, Canada, is remarkable.

As this book has been assembled I am struck with the many questions that remain. Certain paradoxes and wonders of human nature have stood out for me: I have learned of the enormity of my great-great grandfather Robert Sr.'s material legacy (he left behind a true fortune when he died in 1927); at the same time I have learned of the enormity of Robert's piety, which paralleled the growth of his material fortune. I am intrigued by that parallel - that he wrote copiously and passionately about Christianity, while at the same time amassing worldly wealth at an astonishing rate. I am also struck with the fact that George B. Cluett was a renowned philanthropist, contributing to organizations in Troy benefitting youth and the disadvantaged, and was a significant patron of the Grenfell Mission in Labrador, supporting Wilfred's Grenfell's efforts to bring healthcare and mission outreach to Labrador by providing ships. He helped to build the Cluett, Peabody shirt enterprise into a world wide business. And yet Troy was also the site of the first female labour union in 1864 (the Collar Laundry Union); then in 1880 the building housing the Cluett factory burned, due, in the estimation of the fire chief, to 'cheap and nasty architecture'.[3] Luckily the employees (largely women) escaped alive. And while I and many of my distant cousins benefit from the educational and other social and material advantages conferred to us by our Cluett ancestors, I know that the labourers in those factories would not likely have been Cluetts. The Cluetts did indeed excel, but could only do so if the factories had workers. And finally William himself: while part of me is galled by all he did to bury the truth about his past, I cannot help but see that it was a phenomenal act of determination that allowed him to depart from all that he had stood for in England (honour, faithfulness, integrity) in order to get his family to America. I am aware that he must have been beset by a lifelong (however deserved!) battle of conscience.

Historic records, family writings, letters and encounters have all played a role in enlarging the story of so many individuals. Through receiving a copy of the Cluett Cadby letters, I have been given a unique opportunity to see into the lives and the world of my recent ancestors. The letters have yielded insight both into the life of a family, and a period of life in America. While I look at the letters and the family with a particular point of view, each time I read the letters I find new details that could be valuable to others with their own interests to pursue. Much more remains to be discovered with respect to the Cluetts, and to broader social and economic realities, as detailed in these moving accounts exchanged between family members in America and those left behind in England.

1 In his book, *The Gold of Troy,* Robert Cluett IV details the diminishment of that fortune by his branch of the family.

2 My father, Robert Cluett IV, has several of the letters from the correspondence between his grandfather, Robert Cluett Jr. ('Bert'), and Bert's first cousin, Sanford Cluett, about their genealogical research. These letters reveal their friendship, shared appreciation of wine, and dedication to researching family history.

3 https://www.fireengineering.com/leadership/a-destructive-fire-at-troy/

The following Appendices include documents written and gathered by other members of the Cluett family, most of which came to me from Ginny Grogan. The outlooks and the experiences of these family members are reflected in their contributions. Through all of our contributions, what is created as a story and a history constitutes a multi-faceted picture. Another part of this picture is Robert Cluett IV's book, *The Gold of Troy*. Although most of us have not met each other, we are all descended from the one couple, William and Ann Bywater Cluett, who boarded a sailing ship out of Liverpool bound for America in 1850.

Appendices

Appendix A – The 7 Children and 38 Grandchildren of William and Ann Cluett

Appendix B – The Cluetts of Troy – A History by Virginia Horger Grogan

Appendix C – Cluett Bibliography

Appendix D – Early Remembrances of Emily (Emmie) Cadby Henry

Appendix E – John Parmenter Cluett and Gorham Cluett – Letters For Their Family

Appendix F – William Cluett Obituaries from Troy Newspapers, September 19, 1890

Appendix A

The 7 Children and 38 Grandchildren Of William and Ann Cluett

(Dates of death given for children who died before adulthood)

1. Emily Ann (b. 1830) m. John Harford Cadby
   - John W., b. 1852
   - Mary b. 1854
   - Emily b. 1855
   - Elizabeth b. 1857
   - Annie b. 1859
   - Percival b. 1861
   - Florence b. 1863
   - Clara b. 1864
   - George E. b. 1866
   - Lillian b. 1868
   - Amanda b. 1870, *d. 1870*

2. J.W.A. (Alfred) (b. 1834) m. Lillie Bontecou
   - Robbie, b. 1865, *d. 1867*
   - Jessie A., b. 1867
   - Minnie, b. 1867, *d. 1873*
   - Eddie, b. 1868, *d. 1869*
   - Stanley, b. 1871, *d. 1873*
   - Louise B., b. 1873
   - Joseph, b 1876, *d. 1878*

3. Mary Harris (b. 1836) m. Joseph N. Mulford
   (no children)

4. George Bywater (b. 1838) m. Amanda Rockwell Fisher
   - George G., b. 1864, *d. 1864 (with first wife Sarah Golden)*
   - George R., b. 1868, *d. 1868*
   - Walter H., b. 1870
   - Nellie A., b. 1871
   - Bessie Louise, b. 1872, *d. 1873*
   - Ernest H., b.1874
   - George. B. Jr., b. 1876
   - Alfonzo R., b. 1877, *d. 1901*
   - Beatrice, b. 1886

5. Edmund (b. 1840) m. Mary A. Stone
   - Albert E., b. 1872
   - Sanford L., b.1874

6. Frederick (b. 1842) m. Frances A. Bishop
   - Charles Frederick, b. 1866
   - William A., b. 1868, *d. 1868*
   - Harry W., b. 1869, *d. 1869*
   - Frances, B., b. 1870
   - Clarence W., b. 1873
   - Mary E. (Bessie) b. 1877

7. Robert (b. 1844) m. Elizabeth Marchisi
   - Robert Jr (Bert), b. 1869
   - George Alfred (Al), b. 1873
   - Emilie, b. 1875

Researched using the Cluett Family Tree, as maintained by Caryn Cluett Gregg.
To obtain a copy of the family tree, e-mail marjorie@ontariohistory.ca . M.C.S.

Appendix B

The Cluetts of Troy – A History

by Virginia Horger Grogan

I have reproduced this brief history of the Cluetts in Troy as researched and written by Ginny Grogan, c. 1990. Ginny's bibliography lists some good sources to consult. M.C.S.

Sources: (B#) refers to books, articles, etc. in the Cluett Bibliography (Appendix C)
(L#) refers to the Letters.

In June 1850, William Cluett left his home in Birmingham, England with his wife Ann Bywater and six of his seven children: John William Alfred (16 years old), Mary Harris (14), George Bywater (11), Edmund (9), Frederick Henry (8), and Robert (6). The family sailed from Liverpool on the British Ship Catherine and arrived at the Port of New York City on 17 July 1850 (B18). The oldest child, Emily Ann, 20 years old, remained in England.

The Cluetts had planned to travel west when they reached America. However, when they arrived in New York, Ann Cluett was not well. A Roman Catholic priest whom they had met while crossing the Atlantic suggested that they go to Troy, New York, and rest there before completing their journey. Therefore, they boarded one more vessel, the steamboat Empire, and sailed up the Hudson River to the city that would become their permanent home. The passenger list for the Catherine shows two Roman Catholic clergymen: John Doran and D. McNulty. The priest that befriended the Cluetts on board ship had a nephew. Bernard Doran Killan, a thirteen-year old passenger, shares Father Doran's name, suggesting that he may be the nephew, and therefore Father Doran was the priest who recommended the stopover in Troy. However Father McNulty visited the Cluetts in Troy (L9), so either of these fellow passengers may have been the kind priest who sent them to the city that became their beloved home.

WILLIAM CLUETT had been a bookseller in Birmingham. Owing debts, he apparently left suddenly and secretly for America. Letters to his daughter indicate that these debts were eventually paid in full. [*On a close reading of the letters, I suggest that it is possible that the debts may not have been paid in full. M.C.S., 2022*]

Soon after his arrival in America, William joined the Methodist Church and became a lay travelling preacher. His first job was in the grocery business (L4) and he also became a bookkeeper for a short period of time. However, only four years after his arrival in Troy, he opened a book and music store at 76 Congress Street: the business he knew and loved. A Branch store was opened in Albany in May 1858. Piano and organ departments were added in 1865 at which time the book business was discontinued. Alfred (JWA) was a partner with his father until he joined his brother George in the latter's collar-making firm. The music business became known as Cluett and Sons when Edmund and Frederick became partners with their father in 1863. After his wife's death in 1876, William lived first with his daughter Mary Mulford and her husband at 92 Fourth Street, and then with his son Edmund and his wife at 42 Second Street (B3 & B21). He died on 18 September 1890 of a bronchial infection in Saratoga, New York, while at the summer residence of his son Alfred. An obituary in one of the Troy newspapers includes this sentence: "Although his coming to Troy was quiet and unheralded, he left behind him on his death yesterday a name which is in the first rank of those most honored in this city."

The little that is known of ANN BYWATER CLUETT is learned through a letter written to her daughter Emily. She was frequently ill; possibly the consequences of an accident before coming to America (B8). She was a religious woman (her faith in God shows in every letter), she loved her family, and she wrote poetry. She died on 30 January 1876.

EMILY ANN, the oldest Cluett child, remained in England. She lived with (or near) her uncle and aunt, Charles and Mary Bywater Lewis. ("Aunt Lewis", Ann Bywater Cluett's sister, later lived with the Cluetts in Troy after her husband died.) Emily married John Harford Wrighton Cadby on 21 September 1851. Emily and John had ten children: John Wrighton, Mary ("Polly"), Emily, Elizabeth, Annie, Percival, Florence, Clara, George Edmund, and Lillian. William and Ann Cluett never gave up hope that Emily and her family would move to Troy. Emily did visit her parents in about 1865; and her young daughter Mary ("Polly") was visiting in 1862 when the Cluetts' house burned in The Great Fire (L25). In April 1869, George B. Cluett brought three of the Cadby children to Troy: John, Polly and Emmie. John and Polly lived with their grandparents, William and Ann; and Emmie lived with George and his wife Amanda (L39-42). These children were to remain in Troy about a year, at which time their mother would take them back to England. However, they never went back. On 11 October 1870, Emily died a few days after giving birth to her eleventh child. The baby, named Amanda after Emily's sister-in-law, also died. So it was only after death that the beloved oldest daughter joined her parents in Troy. Her remains are buried in Troy's Oakwood Cemetery.

In April of 1871, John Cadby brought his remaining seven children to America and settled in Hudson, New York (B18). Polly kept house for her father and the younger children; Emmie remained with her Uncle George and Aunt Amanda (Mr. and Mrs. George B. Cluett); and Annie went to live with the Rev. and Mrs. Joseph N. Mulford (her Uncle Joseph and Aunt Mary.)

JOHN WILLIAM ALFRED began as a clerk for Maullin and Blanchard when he was seventeen years old. He later became a partner with his father in the music store, but left in 1863 to become a partner with his brother George in the collar firm. In 1863 he married Elizabeth ("Lillie") Bontecou, a cousin of Sarah Golden, George's first wife. Like most of the Cluetts,

Alfred had a musical talent. At one time the Cluett brothers and sister had their own orchestra in which Alfred played the violincello; George, the flute; Edmund, the violin; and Fred, the piano (B20). JWA was said to have one of the finest collections of church hymnals in the country. Several years after his death, Alfred's wife and daughters published a collection of his original hymn tunes.

MARY HARRIS was a leading soprano for years and taught voice lessons until she married the Rev. Joseph Mulford, 2 June 1864. Although Mary and Joseph had no children of their own, one of Mary's letters to her sister Emily mentions a foster child that she and Joseph have taken into their home (L32). There is no further mention of this child. In 1889 Mary and Joseph, who had been rector of Christ Church in Troy, went to southern Florida to establish an Episcopal mission on Lake Worth. Joseph built the first building with the help of his young nephew, Sanford L. Cluett, who accompanied the Mulfords to Florida hoping to improve his poor health. Mary named the new church Bethesda-by-the-Sea. A beautiful tribute to Mary is found in the parish register on the day of her death, 2 April 1915. In part it reads: "Those who knew her could not fail to be influenced for good by her, and though children after the flesh were denied her, many spiritual children rise up and call her blessed."(B4) Joseph too was honored by the church at his death in 1920: "Bethesda-by-the-Sea is his Memorial... He built the church both physically and spiritually."(B4)

GEORGE BYWATER, the Cluett's fourth child, made his entry into the collar industry when he was only sixteen. By 1861 he was a partner in the firm called Maullin, Bigelow and Co. In 1873 the company opened a retail men's furnishing store and soon began the manufacture of shirts to order. On 20 March 1880, a fire destroyed the store, then at 74 Federal Street. "While some of the family watched the disaster, George and the others set out to round up architects and carpenters. A temporary location at 556 Fulton Street was secured the same night, workmen started at once to make the necessary repairs, and by morning the firm was carrying on business as usual in its new location."(B7) A local newspaper ended its article about the fire with this comment: "A cheering sight was the walking of four Cluett brothers down Federal and North-Third Streets about 4 p.m. to their new shop on Fulton Street." (*The Northern Budget*, Troy, N.Y. 26 March 1880) Permanent quarters were soon completed on River Street. The firm was incorporated in 1901 as Cluett, Peabody, and Co. and remained as such until 1985 when the company was bought by West Point Pepperell.

George married Sarah Bontecou Golden in 1863, but she died in childbirth a year later (L31). In 1867 he married Amanda Rockwell Fisher. George Bywater Cluett is remembered not only for his success in business, but also for his many philanthropies. In his day he was considered "a public spirited, liberal and influential citizen"(B16) and a "supporter of all enterprises tending towards necessary local improvement and the preservation of good society".(B12) The house that George bought in 1893 at 59 Second Street is now the home of the Rensselaer County Historical Society.

EDMUND, an accomplished musician, an ardent golfer, and a progressive businessman, was "quiet and unostentatious, warmhearted, and liberal" (B13). He began working in his father's store when he was seventeen, and became a partner in 1863. He married Mary Alice Stone in 1871 and they had two sons: Albert Edmund and Sanford Lockwood. Edmund died 10 December 1908.

FREDERICK HENRY became a partner in his father's music and book business, Cluett and Sons, in 1863. He possessed unusual musical talent and was noted as a skilled performer on the piano and pipe organ. At sixteen he was organist at Dr. Magoon's church in Albany. Beginning in 1860 he was the organist and the State Street Methodist Church in Troy for thirty-five years. Several days before his marriage to Frances Amelia Bishop (11 Jan 1866), there was a fire at the Bishop house. Although most of the wedding clothes of the bride and her family were burned, the wedding went off as scheduled, and was followed by a trip to Europe, the gift of Fannie's father. Frederick died 23 December 1909 (B13).

ROBERT, the youngest of the Cluett children, worked as a clerk for Maullin and Blanchard in 1862. He became a partner of the firm (the George B. Cluett, Bros., and Co.) in 1866. After incorporation, Robert was vice-president of the firm (1901-1902) and then president (1902-1907). Robert was interested in politics, and was an alderman representing Troy's third ward from 1886-1890 (B21). He married Elizabeth Marchisi ("Lizzie"), 19 May 1868, and they had three children: Robert Jr., George Alfred, and Emily Josephine. Lizzie died 30 April 1916, and he married a widow, Mrs. Emily R. Webster on 1 August 1917. Robert died at Hubbard Woods, Illinois 25 Nov 1927.

These seven children of William and Ann Cluett produced 27 children who lived beyond childhood. By 1990, their descendants numbered five hundred.

Virginia (Ginny) Grogan
1990

Appendix C

Cluett Bibliography

by Virginia Horger Grogan

[*Most of this research was done by Ginny before the internet was available! M.C.S.*]

1. *Biographical Directory of the American Congress: 1774-1971.* The U.S. Government Printing Office, 1971.

2. *Brewster Genealogy 1566-1907.* The Grafton Press, 1908. (Includes information about Annah Robinson Cluett)

3. Census Records 1850-1910: Federal Center, Denver, CO.

4. *Chronicles 1889-1964: 175th Anniversary publication of the Church of Bethesda-by-the Sea, Palm Beach, FL.* Palm Beach, FL: Distinctive Printing, Inc., 1964

5. "The Cluett Family... Genealogy" ('The name occurs first in Staffordshire in the year 1327') Duplicated and compiled by John Parmenter Cluett and Gorham Cluett (brothers), and their mother, Margaret Gorham Cluett: Christmas 1964.

[*M.C.S. — A number of the Cluett genealogies have errors, including one commissioned by Robert Cluett Jr. and Sanford Lockwood Cluett (first cousins) in the 1930's (possibly the one referenced here), and distributed in the family.* *See Epilogue, pages 178 to 179.*]

6. "The Cluett Family... Letters." Duplicated and compiled by John Parmenter Cluett and Gorham Cluett (brothers), and their mother. V.H.G. had photocopies of the eight letters; the originals were held by Ellen (Cluett) Burnham; some are now in the Hart Cluett Museum (2021).

7. "The Curious Mr. Cluett": an article about Sanford Cluett by Floyd Tifft, *Alumni News*, Rensselaer Polytechnic Institute, Jan. 1947.

8. "Diary of Amanda Rockwell Cluett (1900-1917)." Donated to the Rensselaer County Historical Society, Troy, NY, by Robert Cluett Black III

9. "Early Remembrances of Emily Cadby Henry." Handwritten notes in the possession of Ellen (Cluett) Burnham. 1936?

10. "George Bywater Cluett 1832-1912": a paper written by J. Lawrence Meader and read by him at the meeting of the Rensselaer County Historical Association on 10 Jan. 1940.

11. *Gregory Stone Genealogy*. J. Gardner Bartlett. Boston: Published for the Stone Family Association, 1918. (Includes information about Mary Alice Stone.)

12. *History of the City of Troy*. A.J Weise, M.A., Troy: William H. Young, 1876.

13. *History of Rensselaer County, New York*. Nathanial Bartlett Sylvester. New York: Everts & Peck, 1880.

14. *Hudson-Mohawk Genealogical and Family Memoirs*, Volume II, edited by Cuyler Reynolds. New York: Lewis Historical Publishing Company, 1911.

15. *Hymns with Original Tunes*. J.W.A. Cluett. Edwin S. Gorham, publisher, 1904. 100 copies printed for private circulation.

16. "Kin-Tree: a listing of the descendants of William and Ann Bywater Cluett." Assembled by Emily (Dorlon) Rodemann, February. 1985. Walter Stetson Cluett had a hand in this also.
[*Note: This Cluett family genealogy has since been digitized and maintained by Caryn Cluett Gregg of California. For access to a copy, e-mail: marjorie@ontario-history.ca*]

17. *Landmarks of Rensselaer County, New York*. George Baker Anderson. Syracuse, NY: D. Mason & Co., 1897.

18. *Refugees of 1776 from Long Island to Connecticut*. Frederic Gregory Mather. Baltimore: Genealogical publishing Co., 1972. (Information about the Bontecou family).

19. *A Resourceful People: A Pictorial History of Rensselaer County, New York*. By 7 people for the Rensselaer County Historical Society. Norfolk, VA: The Donning Company Publishers, 1987.

20. "Ship Passenger Lists: 1850, 1869, 1871." Federal Archives, Washington, D.C.

21. "Shyne Collection of Newspaper Clippings." In possession of heirs of Lydia Cluett Shyne Plaut.

22. *Troy and Rensselaer County, New York*, Vols. I, II, III. Rutherford Hayner, published 1925.

23. *Troy City Directories*.

24. Troy's *One Hundred Years: 1789-1889*. Arthur James Weise, M.A.

25. *Who was Who in America*, Vol. 1 (1897-1942), Vol. 3 (1960), Vol. V (1969-1973) Chicago: A.N. Marquis Company.

Valuable information was also contributed by:

Robert C. Black III
Ellen Cluett Burnham
Marvin V. (Pete) Cluett
Robert Cluett IV
Walter S. Cluett
Martha (Dorlon) Mitchell
Lydia Cluett (Shyne) Plaut
Emily (Dorlon) Rodemann
Rensselaer County Historical Society

V.H.G. 1990

Appendix D

Early Remembrances
Of Emily (Emmie) Cadby Henry
c.1936

Emily Cadby Henry (b. 1855) was the daughter of Emily Cluett Cadby (b. 1830). This is Emmie's description of the life of her mother, Emily, who died after childbirth at age forty, when Emmie was fifteen. This text was distributed by Ginny Grogan

I have reproduced these notes as composed; there are some factual errors, but the document here is as originally written in 1936. Words or phrases in square brackets [ ] are my notes. M.C.S.

"The story of my Mother's life" — The oldest member of the Cluett children of my Grandfather and Grandmother William and Anne Cluett.

When my Mother Emily Cluett was fifteen years old, her Mother [Ann] met with an accident. She was attending an auction sale when the floor on which she was standing gave way precipitating every onto the floor below — my Grandmother was so seriously hurt that she became an invalid for the rest of her life. [*In the Cluett Cadby letters, Ann is well enough to do housework, oversee hired help, go for walks and care for the gardens.*] My Mother being the eldest of the family took entire charge of the household which consisted of her Father, one sister, Mary, five brothers: Alfred, George, Edmund, Fred and Robert; the latter a baby six months old — quite a task for a girl of fifteen years of age. She must have proven equal to the task of caring for this baby- as well as the care of her Father, her brothers and sister as my Grandfather in after years so often told me all she had meant to him during the five years before they came to America when the baby Robert was five years old. Those five years when his sister Emily had been a Mother in every sense of the word to him. My Mother was engaged to be married to John Hearford Wrighton Cadby, so remained in England with her Aunt Lewis — her Mother's sister — Emily was 20 years old but had promised her father she would not marry until she was 21.

My father [John Cadby] had a large book store of rare and old books. It was doing well. My grandfather and G'Mother, Mr. and Mrs. William Cluett left England with one daughter, Mary, and five sons, telling no one when or where he was going as he was greatly in debt. My Father [John Cadby] suffered for years from this as he was obliged to pay those debts of his Father-in-law before he could go on with his business. No one would deal with him until he did. My Mother so often talked to me about this as they suffered greatly for some years. He was really boycotted.

When I was five years old and recovering from scarlet fever [*1860 or 1861*], sitting by an open fire one day, my sister Pollie came running to me saying that Uncle Edmund has come all the way from America to see us. He was the first of my Mother's family to come back to England. On returning to America, he took Pollie back for a visit to see her Grandmother. She remained a year, when Aunt Mary brought her back. After that, Mother's brothers and sisters visited us quite often — This was after all debts had been paid by my Father [*John Cadby*]. [*In the Cluett letters, it is clear that many debts remained to be paid beyond those that John and Emily Cadby covered themselves.*]

In 1869 Uncle George and Aunt Amanda came to see us and persuaded my Mother to let them take my oldest brother John and sister Pollie and myself back with them for a visit, that my Grandmother was so desirous to see us. I was to remain a year when my Mother would come to

America for me. During that year my Mother passed away so I never went back. My Mother had eleven children: eight girls and three boys. My Mother died with her eighth girl. A year after my Mother's death, my Father brought the children to America. All married in this country: Mary Cluett (Pollie), Dr. Brelsford; Emily, the Rev. Ha. Ashton Henry; Elizabeth, John Forshew; Annie, Marvin E. Stowe; Florence, Edwain W. Elmore; Clara never married; Lily, the youngest [*named for Aunt Lillie*], Philip S. Dorlon. Poor, all of them, but good women everyone.

Grandfather and Grandmother Cluett with their six children sailed for America in the year 1849 [*1850*]. Grandfather had planned to go West, but a priest on the ship persuaded him to go to a city called Troy before deciding on a place to settle. They remained in Troy.

During the visit of Pollie, the big fire occurred on June 10th 1862. Up to that time the family had lived somewhere up town. My Grandfather keeping a book store, the children attending public school until the boys were old enough to earn their living. My Aunt Mary having a beautiful voice taught singing and both she and her brother George sang in churches both in Albany and Troy. After the fire, George being the business man of the family, joined the business of Maullin and Bigelow collar manufacturers — the business of which in after years he became its head. The family after the fire moved down on First Street where they lived for several years.

When George became the head of his collar business, he offered his brother Alfred a position as travelling salesman. As Alfred being of a literary nature was not earning his salt and never would have. As I remember he was not a success at that, so his brother George gave him a position in the Factory as bookkeeper where he remained the rest of his life. Robert also later joined the firm of Geo B. Cluett Brother and Co. and was a very active and useful member.

I can remember so well when Uncle Robert was living on Pawling Ave. opposite the skating park and his son Alfred was a tiny baby — I used to nearly always take Sunday night suppers with them. He would say – "Emmie when I am worth a hundred thousand dollars, if I ever am, I shall retire from business," and as he was so small he would straighten himself up and look fairly tall.*

Emily Cadby Henry

These remembrances were written by Emily (Cadby) Henry in later life. The original handwritten notes are in the possession of Ellen (Gorham Cluett) Burnham (c. 1964).

Emily Cadby Henry. b. 30 Nov 1855, d. 15 Dec. 1943
m. 27 April 1887, The Rev. H. Ashton Henry.
Their only child, Madeleine Amanda, 1887-1967, never married.

* Robert evidently became worth much more than $100,000. One of his donations alone, towards the land and building of the first Troy Y.M.C.A., totalled $140,000. According to his great-grandson (Robert Cluett IV), Robert left an estate worth 12 million dollars at his death in 1927.

Appendix E

John Parmenter Cluett and Gorham Cluett

Letters for Their Family, 1964

Editorial remark: The preamble below was written by two of George B. Cluett's grandsons in 1964, when they duplicated a set of the eight Cluett Cadby letters they had in their possession, to distribute to their family members. Their awareness of the material and social legacy of their Cluett family is clear in these notes.

I have included their preamble, although the set of 43 letters published in this book is more complete than the 8 they had, and tells more of the story of the Cluetts, but they include some additional family history here. I do not have the news clippings to which they refer.

I am from the Robert Cluett line, and never met John P. (JPC) or Gorham (GC). For their care in helping to preserve the letters, I am grateful. Bracketed, italicized phrases are my editorial notes. M.C.S.

Preamble. Christmas 1964

John Parmenter Cluett [*JPC*] and Gorham Cluett [*GC*], eldest and youngest sons of Ernest Harold Cluett, and Margaret Gorham Cluett, have duplicated and compiled these two volumes, respectively — "The Cluett Family - Geneology" and "the Cluett Family - Letters - News Clippings - Pictures." Gorham Cluett or his heirs have the original Geneology and the original letters.[1]

Because the Geneology ended with George Bywater Cluett it is our conclusion that he had it done by a firm in England; although Sanford L. Cluett, son of Edmund, being a great family historian, may have done it or had it done for his uncle, George. [2]

Our gratitude goes to all our living relatives who have helped with this venture, particularly our Auntie Bee, Beatrice Cluett (Black), the only living member of that generation other than Sanford L. Cluett who, at this writing, is 90 years old, is still a vice-president of the family business, Cluett, Peabody and Company, and is the inventor not only of the famous Sanforizing Process (non-shrinkable fabrics) but also of extensible paper, trade-marked Clupak.

Letter #1 [*letter #2 in this book*] June 26, 1850, Emily to William.

This letter written 115 years ago by Emily Cluett, who was 20 years old when her father, mother, sister and five brothers suddenly left a bankrupt bookstore, owned by William Cluett, in Wolverhampton, England, and set forth in a sailing vessel from Liverpool to America. The ages of the eight adventurers follow: William, 44; Ann Bywater, 39; John William Alfred, 16; Mary Harris, 14; George Bywater, 12; Edmund, 10; Frederick Henry, 8; Robert, 6.

The only conclusion we two great-grandchildren of William and Ann Bywater can draw is that Emily was in love with John Herford W. Cadby, who worked in William Cluett's bookstore, and she chose to remain behind in spite of all the adversity inherent in this sad letter. Indeed, Emily did marry John Cadby a year later, in 1851, and before she died 19 years later, in 1870, she and John had 11 children of whom more later.

As to any debts that William Cluett left unpaid in England, a full reading of this volume [*the eight letters in their possession*] will convince the most skeptical that it is simply inconceivable that in view of the tremendous moral, religious and financial responsibility of this entire family that any money owed to anyone here or abroad was not eventually paid in full. [*see "A View of William Cluett and his Debt," page 155 above*].

Emily's letter, addressed "Mr. William Cluett, Post Office, New York, North America" was returned stamped "Sent back to England without a reason for non-delivery." Where you find "...." in the typed copy portions of the original are missing with age.

Letter #2 [*letter #3 in this book*] Ann to Emily, June 26, 1850, while at sea.

Note the sentence beginning, "I know not what I should have done—". The "Catholic Priest" referred to was returning to his parish, St. Joseph's Seminary in Troy, N.Y, and it was he who persuaded William and Ann Bywater Cluett, the latter still exhausted from the effects of the storm-tossed, 37-day trip, to go up the Hudson River with their six children and settle in Troy before venturing further west as they had planned.

Toward the end of this letter, "Give my kind love to John—" underscores the conclusion we reached as to why Emily did not accompany her family to America.

Letter #3 [*letter #15 in the book*] JW Alfred to Emily, March 1, 1854.

This letter to Emily Cluett (Cadby), from her eldest brother, John William Alfred, was written when he was 20 years old. He was at the time a clerk for the collar firm of Maullin and Blanchard, as was his brother, George Bywater, age 16.

Imagine in this day and age a yearly salary of $400 and stating "…I can live very comfortably on that and still save a little also."

Of all the letters in this volume [*eight letters*] this is by far the most amusing, particularly when JWA refers to all his younger brothers.

This letter to Emily (Cluett) Cadby has to be from Mary Harris Cluett (her only sister). The reference to Chatham is Chatham, N.Y., about twenty-five miles southeast of Troy, but who the "country cousins" are we have no idea. "Canaan" is a few miles east of Chatham.

My (JPC) earliest record of Aunt Mary Cluett (Mulford) and her husband (despite her statement, "… poor me, will I am afraid always have to look after myself,") Joseph N. Mulford was probably in about 1905 when they lived in a small cottage nearby Grandpa's (George B. Cluett's) big summer house in Saratoga, N.Y. Aunt Mary would have been almost seventy then and I recall her being tiny in stature, with twinkling eyes and quick-as-a-wink humor. As a small boy Uncle Joseph used to take me on "long" walks through the woods on the "Indian Trails" — an experience I will never forget, accompanied by this fine, lovable, God-fearing man.

It was Uncle Joseph (an Episcopal clergyman) who took Sanford L. Cluett to Palm Beach, Florida (then called Lake Worth), because of the latter's poor health as a young lad; and it was those two together who built the first church there, in 1889 known then, as now in its present magnificence, as Bethesda-by-the-Sea. In fact an examination of the underside of the pews at the time would have attested to the fact that they had been made of boards of wooden crates washed up on the beach — why else would SCOTCH WHISKEY be stamped on the bottom of the pews? *[I visited this church in 1994 and the Whiskey stamp was still visible. M.C.S.]*

In these early days the train only ran as far south as Titusville, Florida. From there a mail boat took what few passengers there were as far as Jupiter where they changed to a smaller boat that continued on down the inland waterway to Palm Beach.

[There is no Letter #4 in this group.]

Letter #5 [*#24 in this book*] July 8, 1862, William to Emily.

In this letter to Emily Cluett (Cadby) from her father, William, we find that in may 1858, William Cluett, having opened his first store in Troy in 1854, opened a branch music and book store in Albany, N.Y., with two of his sons, John William Alfred, and Frederick Henry. From old news clippings further along in this volume [*not in my possession*] we find that while JWA was with Maullin and Blanchard in 1854, he left the collar business to join his father and brother, Frederick, in the music and book store in 1858.

In 1862, due to the death or retirement of the original partners, the collar firm became Maullin and Cluett (George B. Cluett). Mr. Maullin died in 1863 and George B. Cluett called in as his partner, John William Alfred, who left Cluett and Son (the music store). The collar firm thereupon became George B. Cluett, Brother and Co. In 1866 a third brother, Robert, entered the firm (see details in news clippings further on) [*not in this book*].

On p.3 of this letter it is interesting to note that "George is still in the collar business, but will leave it and come into one of the (music) stores next spring." It is evident that in 1858 the music business was doing far better for the musical Cluetts than Maullin and Blanchard (collars and cuffs) was for George B. Cluett. How completely different the family fortunes might have been if George B. Cluett had gone into the music business as his father intimates above.

We also note on p.3 of the letter that Edmund the only son so far unaccounted for "..had to leave the hardware business to come into the Troy (music) store with me."

The reference on the last page of the letter to "your aunt and uncle Lewis" clears up a controversial point, i.e., that the large family photograph inserted further on in this volume [*on the cover of this book*], and taken about 1867, contains a picture (marked 12) of "Aunt Lewis." She was more than "a friend," being Ann Bywater Cluett's sister, Mary Bywater (Lewis) who presumably came over from England to join the rest of the family in Troy, when her husband, Charles Lewis, died. She was born in 1811, died in 1876 and is buried in the old Cluett lot in Oakwood Cemetery.

In the last paragraph note William Cluett's desire to have his daughter, Emily, and her family come to join him in America.

Letter #6 [*letter #31 in this book*] November 14, 1864 George to Emily.

This extremely heart-rending letter, written almost exactly 100 years ago to Emily Cluett (Cadby), 34 years old, by her brother, George B. Cluett, 26, really emphasizes how much he would love to have some of his sister's children come over from England to live with him.

The mention of "gold at 240" vs "gold at 150" is simply a matter of inflation during the Civil War then in progress.

Our grandfather, George B. Cluett, following the tragic death of his first wife, Sarah Golden, has gone to live with his sister, Mary, who has married the Rev. Joseph N. Mulford, as stated earlier.

Further along in this letter you will note George's insistence in having at least one of his sister Emily's children when he says "... you must make up your mind to part with one of the children for I do not intend to return alone..."

Letter #7-A [*letter #40 in this book*] September 3, 1869 George to Emily and John.

George B. Cluett and his wife Amanda Rockwell Cluett have finally persuaded John and Emily to part with their three eldest children: John Jr., Mary (Polly) and Emily (Emmie) with the understanding that their mother will come over from England in one year and pick them up.

Note with reference to the Geneology and the date of this letter that when it was written, Sept. 3, 1869, Amanda Rockwell Cluett was heavy with Walter Herbert. She had one previous child, George Rockwell, who died and about 1873, another Bessie Louise who also died.

Letter #7-B [*letter #43 in this book*] Amanda to Emily November 7, 1869.

When this letter was written by Amanda Rockwell Cluett to her sister-in-law, Emily Cluett (Cadby), Emmie as 14 years old.

The "family gathering at Alfred's..." is JWA Cluett, and his wife, Lillie.

"Edmund is still in Albany...." see Letter #5 [*letter #23 in this book*]
"He is still attentive to a young lady there" possibly his future wife, May Alice Stone (Cluett) mother of Sanford L. and Albert E. Cluett.

On page two, the reference to John (Cadby Jr.) speaks for itself.

Amanda, toward the end of p.2 of this letter, mentions the hope that her husband, George (B. Cluett), will become a farmer! (Rather than what eventually became the largest collar firm in the world? JPC/ GC.)

"I am afraid Emmie will never accomplish much with her needle." I (JPC) can remember visiting Aunt Emmie and Uncle Ashton Henry in Saratoga about 1906 and she let me, aged 6, do some hemming on dish towels, so maybe her Aunt Amanda, my grandmother, was correct in giving Emmie "the needle" about her sewing ability!

On p.3, "Fred and Fannie agree about as usual..." speaks for itself. "Freddie" is their son.

"...spare Flora for me," is a remarkable show of affection from our grandmother, Amanda, who has just brought three of the Cadby children over from England and was, at this writing, soon to have a child of her own.

Letter #8 [*This letter, from George B. Cluett to his heirs, is not in this book.*]

All of the desires of George B. Cluett, expressed in this wonderful letter to his "dear Wife and Children," were carried out to the letter. Annie Kelly was their laundress; George B. Wells, first the coachman and later the family chauffeur; Henry Burdo, the butler, with his wife, Harriet, several years after this letter was written, the chambermaid.

We two brothers, grandchildren of George B. Cluett, urgently suggest that not only our children but our grandchildren and their children and their grandchildren shall emulate their beloved ancestor George B. Cluett, particularly in respect to his reverent desires set for the in paragraphs #6 and #9:

> "Just as long as you are able to do so, I trust that you will all be ready to assist in all philanthropic work, and in all the years to come, may our family reputation in

this regard be fully maintained. Give generously to every good cause; help such as are needy or in distress, setting such an example in this respect as shall be emulated by others.

"Most devoutly and reverently do I give thanks and praise to my Heavenly Father for all the gifts and blessings with which my life has been filled. And now to His care and keeping do I commit my dear wife and children. Give your hearts and lives to Him and through His infinite love and mercy that we may all meet again and become an unbroken family in the 'House of Many Mansions' is the loving, fervent prayer of your affectionate husband and father. George B. Cluett"[3]

[*GC and JPC preamble continues:*] These God-given qualities in a man, unfortunately, are getting scarcer and scarcer with the passage of time; and though future generations of our family may scan this volume from cover to cover, they will find no greater legacy than has been handed down to them than the words and thoughts expressed in these two inspiring paragraphs.

George B. Cluett and Amanda Cluett. c.1900
[Caryn Cluett Gregg collection]

Postscript [*by Gorham Cluett and John Parmenter Cluett*]

Just 11 months after letter #7-B was written [*letter #43 in this book*], Emily Cluett (Cadby's) 11th child, Amanda (named for Emily's sister-in-law, Amanda Rockwell Cluett) died at birth and the mother died a few days later, Oct. 10, 1870. Her remains were eventually brought from England to Troy and interred in the old Cluett lot in Oakwood Cemetery.

John Harford W. Cadby soon brought his seven other children to the United States and settled in Hudson, N.Y. The children were Elizabeth, Annie, Percy, Florence, Clara, George Edmund and Lillian. Polly (see Letter # 7-A)[*letter #26*] kept house for her father. Emmie remained with her Uncle George and Aunt Amanda (Mr. and Mrs. George B. Cluett) and Annie went to live with the Rev. and Mrs. Joseph N. Mulford (Mary Harris Cluett).

In due course but not necessarily in order the sisters married and became Polly Brelsford, Lizzie Forshew, Annie Stow, Flo Elmore and Lil Dorlon. No data is available on the other Cadby children.

Of special interest is Aunt Emmie [*Cadby*] who, as related above, lived with our grandfather and grandmother, George B. and Amanda Rockwell Cluett. Indeed, from 1869 until Sept. 4, 1959 (the death of Nellie Agnes Cluett), Emmie Cadby and later her husband, Rev. H Ashton Henry, and finally their daughter, Madeleine Amanda Henry, were as close to our grandfather and grandmother and Aunt Nellie as if they had been sister, brother, and daughter. The inception of this mutual love and attachment dates back 90 years as of this writing.

A house on 8th Street in Troy was basically the first homestead of George B. and Amanda R. Cluett; then, later, they moved to 3 Park Place. In 1893 the family moved to 59 Second Street (presently The Troy Historical Society). The same year grandpa followed his brother-in-law's example (Rev. Joseph. N. Mulford) and spent the winters on the edge of Lake Worth in Palm Beach, Florida. In 1905, he built a beautiful mansion at the same location and spent seven wonderful winters there until his death at 59 Second Street, Troy, N.Y., in 1912. The house was soon sold by our grandmother.

Our own father, Ernest Harold Cluett, and mother moved into 60 Second Street after they were married in 1899 and that's where I (JPC) was born. We soon moved out of the city proper into the outskirts, 28 Locust Avenue, where William Gorham was born and then Gorham Cluett.

In 1910 our father, Ernest Harold Cluett, built a magnificent Elizabethan house on Pinewoods Avenue adjoining the Emma Willard School. Our three sisters were born there. The following year our grandfather started building a beautiful Colonial house next door to us. He never lived long enough to move in. His daughter, Beatrice Cluett, married R. Clifford Black about a year after her father's death which left our grandmother and Aunt Nellie the sole occupants of the new house.

It was then that the Rev. H. Ashton Henry and his wife, Emily Cadby (Henry) and their only child, Madeleine A. Henry, came to live with Grandma and Aunt Nell. Grandma died in 1918. Uncle Ashton Henry died in 1920. Aunt Emmie (Henry) died in 1943. Their daughter, Madeleine, remained to run the household for Nellie A. Cluett until the latter's death in 1959, aged 87.

Our house and property had been donated to the Emma Willard School upon mother's death in 1943. Grandmother's house and property (left to Nellie A. Cluett for life occupancy) was sold to Emma Willard School. Madeleine Henry and Catherine Requa Cluett, our father's second wife of only a few years, bought a house on Westover Road, N. Y., and are living there at this writing.

A careful reading of the old news clippings that follow [*not in this book*] will document the purposeful lives, the business integrity, the charitable works and religious and civic responsibilities of the Cluett family before us.

We, the compilers of this volume, hope and pray that some one of our children, mindful of his great heritage, will, in due course, continue the story of the Cluett Family where we have left off.

John Parmenter Cluett, Gorham Cluett, Christmas, 1964

1 See 'Epilogue — Letters, Genealogies and Encounters' in this book.

2 See 'Epilogue — Letters, Genealogies and Encounters' in this book.

3 Paragraphs read from George B's letter at a Cluett family reunion in 1996, by Nancy Cluett Burroughs. Courtesy of Caryn Cluett Gregg.

Appendix F

William Cluett Obituaries

From Troy Newspapers, September 19, 1890

William Cluett (Obituary #1)

William Cluett, of Cluett & Sons, the music dealers of this city, died at 7 o'clock last evening at the summer residence of his son, J.W.A. Cluett, in Saratoga, of a bronchial affection. He had been ill only about a week and his death was not expected.

William Cluett was truly a representative Trojan. Such worldly interests as he was possessed of are centred in our city. His wealth was here accumulated, and by his example, energy and business qualification he has in days past created business of value to our city as well as remunerative to himself. His transmitted qualifications as business man and loyal citizen are shown in the vast business conducted by his sons. The largest collar factory in Troy, employing hundreds of well paid employés, is owned by three of his sons, while others of his sons conduct a large music emporium in this city. Mr. Cluett has ever been ready to respond to calls for charity, or for contribution to funds for the improvement of educational and other beneficial institutions in Troy. His life had been that of a pure unpretentious Christian, blameless before the world. Mr. Cluett was born in the village of Hilton, Staffordshire, Eng., in the year 1806, and received his education in the grammar school of Bridgeworth, Eng. His first efforts at labor were as schoolmaster, and later as civil engineer.

While still a young man he became deeply impressed with the tenets of the society of Methodists, following in the belief and creed of his father and grandfather, and as a result he became well known as an earnest and most successful local preacher. He made his first commercial venture in the book business and carried on that business until his emigration to this country in 1850. In that year he came to Troy with his family and resided at No. 168 Fifth street, being employed as a clerk and bookkeeper at No. 214 River street.

In 1855 he opened a bookstore at No.75 Congress street, being a pioneer in that business in this city. In a few years he removed his store to No. 266 River street, where, under the firm name of Wm. Cluett & Son, he largely increased his stock of books, etc., and added to his business an extensive and successful agency for pianos and sheet music. Later a branch store was established in Albany, and for many years Mr. Cluett had the ability to successfully conduct this business, increasing it year by year until his health forbade further business cares and he retired from active business life. Mr. Cluett never attempted to enter public life, his likings and tastes inducing him to seek the quiet and peace of home and its surrounding comforts. An extensive reader and very able judge of fine books and rare editions, he collected a valuable library and enjoyed his life among his family and his books. He was a reader of the true form and acquired an extended and valuable knowledge of books and their contents. One of his "hobbies" (all book lovers have a hobby) of Mr. Cluett in the book line was works on angling, of which he had many valuable specimens. A great lover of the sport, he had practical knowledge of its nice points and enjoyed it as only a true sportsman and lover of nature can enjoy it. Quiet and retiring in his manner, an earnest Christian, charitable, generous and lenient to those who fail to live up to the standard of duty, his own life was blameless. Having passed the "three score and ten" allotment of life's years and reached the age of 83, it is a proud record to leave for his children, that in all those long years there be naught but good recorded.

The deceased had not been in the best of health for several years but it was the feebleness resulting from old age. He spent last winter in Florida, but did not gain in strength. The summer had been passed by him at Saratoga and on the shores of Lake Champlain, as had been his habit for many years. On Sunday evening last, he was seized with a chill, but the first serious results were noticed yesterday, and he sank rapidly until he died. Around his bedside at the last moments were his five sons,

George B., J.W.A. and Robert Cluett of the shirt and collar firm of Cluett, Coon & Co, Fred. H. and Edmund Cluett of Cluett & Sons, music dealers. Besides the sons, there is one daughter, Mrs. J. N. Mulford, wife of Rev. J.N. Mulford, formerly rector of Christ Church in this city. She is now in the Adirondack mountains, where she has been spending the summer, and has been telegraphed for. Mr. Cluett was a widower, his wife having died in January, 1876. For many years the deceased had been a prominent member of the State street Methodist church, from which the funeral will take place at 11 o'clock Monday morning.

William Cluett (Obituary #2)

Forty years ago there came to this city a man who had been a bookseller in England. He came to seek in this land a comfortable living for himself and his family. He brought with him willing hands, a clear head, a mind well stored with information and disciplined by study and careful observation of life, and, above all, a character of inflexible uprightness. Although his coming to Troy was quiet and unheralded, he left behind him on his death yesterday a name which is in the first rank of those most honored in this city.

This man was William Cluett, and his death at Saratoga yesterday causes widespread grief, as well as expressions of unstinted admiration. The most memorable thing about William Cluett, and that which was the foundation of all his worthy life, was the purity of his heart and the integrity of his intentions. He meant to do business, but he meant to do it in such a way as would help and not hinder his fellow men, and preserve his own reputation as one whose purposes were loftier than selfish aggrandizement and whose aims were higher than merely temporal possessions.

Mr. Cluett was fortunate in her who, as his wife, shared his efforts and his successes. His business career, including as it did an advancement from humble beginnings in the sale of books and musical wares to the establishment of one of the largest music houses in the country, is a lesson for the youth of to-day. But with his business activity and his personal success, Mr. Cluett always united that singularly warm domestic affection which made his children's fortunes inseparably allied to his own, so that when one thinks of the credit which attaches to this pure, straightforward, even-handed life, there springs to mind instantly the thought not only of William Cluett, but of the Cluett family — a group of strong men and noble, pure-minded women, whose influence in this city has been a notable factor in securing its advancement not only commercial and industrial progress but in the finer departments of moral and aesthetic improvement.

William Cluett, c. 1875.
[Courtesy of the Hart Cluett Museum, Troy, N.Y]

These two obituaries were in the set of photocopies distributed by Ginny Grogan; I do not know in which Troy newspapers they were published. *M.C.S.*

List of Sources

Material from Virginia (Ginny) Horger Grogan

• Cluett Cadby letters (42), copies transcribed by Virginia Horger Grogan (V.H.G.), received 2015. Originals of these letters viewed by M.C.S. in the Hart Cluett Museum (H.C.M.), Troy, N.Y., 2021

• "Recollections of Emily Cadby Henry", photocopy courtesy V.H.G.

• "Preamble", John Parmenter Cluett and Gorham Cluett, 1964; photocopy courtesy V.H.G.

• William Cluett obituaries; Troy newspapers, 1890

• Research summary "The Cluetts of Troy, A History"; Bibliography and Listing of Letters,V.H.G.

• Handwritten R.S.V.P. note by Lillie Bontecou Cluett

• 'Dorlon-Moore-Cluett Cadby – How their descendants found happiness in Rensselaer County'; The Family Newsletters, 1981-1985, Virginia Horger Grogan and Emily Rodemann

• Phone conversations with Virginia (Ginny) Horger Grogan (2019-2022)

Material from Robert Cluett IV

• *The Gold of Troy*, Robert Cluett, Discourse Associates, 2003; *Tailings from The Gold of Troy*, Robert Cluett, Discourse Associates, 2017

• Family photos from and conversations with Robert Cluett IV

• Correspondence between and genealogy research of Robert Cluett Jr. and Sanford L. Cluett, 1930's, Robert Cluett IV archives

• Hand-drawn Cluett Genealogy, c. 1890's; Hardbound Cluett Genealogy, c. 1940's

Material from the Hart Cluett Museum/ Rensselaer Historical Society

• Troy City Directories, 1850-1869

• John Warner Barber and Henry Howe, *Historical Collections of the State of New York*, 1851

• Cluett and Sons Music Co. Catalogue, c. 1902, Introduction by Frederick Cluett Jr.

• Diary of Amanda Rockwell Cluett, 1900-1917 (wife of George B. Cluett), original in the Hart Cluett Museum; photocopy courtesy of the H.C.M/ Rensselaer County Historical Society

• The Marble House tour of the museum with historian Kathy Sheehan; identifying of Robert Cluett Jr. and Amy Knight Cluett portraits with archivist Stacey Pomeroy Draper

• A.J. Weise, *The City of Troy and Its Vicinity, 1886*

• A.J. Weise, *History of the City of Troy*, 1876
Also at: https://archive.org/details/historyofcityoft01weis/page/209/mode/2up

• A.J. Weise, *Troy's One Hundred Years*, 1889
Also at: https://archive.org/details/troysonehundredy00weis

Material from Caryn Cluett Gregg

• Family tree, initiated by Emily Rodemann and Walter S. Cluett (c. 1980); digitized (now in MS-Excel format) and maintained by Caryn Cluett Gregg.
For a copy of this family tree, email marjorie@ontariohistory.ca

• Family photos and documents from the George B. Cluett line, courtesy Caryn Cluett Gregg

• Visit with fourth cousins Caryn Cluett Gregg and T.G. Williams (from the George B. Cluett line), and Barbara Cluett William's husband, Tom Williams, in California at her memorial service in 2017.

Courtesy of Helen Curry Cluett

• *The History of Methodism In Troy*, Joseph Hillman, 1888; digitized by Cornell University. Includes photographs of (Reverend) William Cluett and all five sons, reproduced here.

Index

Biographies

AUTHOR — **Marjorie Cluett Seguin** was born in Connecticut, the middle daughter of Robert Cluett IV and Thayer McMillan Bodman. The family migrated to Toronto, Canada, in 1967 and Marjorie did all of her schooling in Canada. In this line of the Cluett family, there is just one Cluett first cousin, Catherine Belden Nail, and no Cluett second cousins. Marjorie has two Cluett siblings (Helen Cluett and Holly Gwynne-Timothy), and a third sibling, cousin Amy Bodman, who became part of the family in the 1970's. Marjorie's sense of family was expanded as a result of the death of the parents of Amy and her sisters, which led to a broader and more interconnected family web.

Marjorie trained as an art teacher in Nova Scotia, and taught art in schools in Newfoundland and in Toronto. She later founded a community art school in Toronto, before moving to Prince Edward County, Ontario, with her young family in 2002.

In recent decades, she has joined Thayer Cluett, Rosamond Bailey, and Marjorie's three siblings in forming Two Fishes Press, to reflect on and write about Christianity.

Marjorie lives in Prince Edward County, Ontario, with her husband, Marc Seguin. They have two sons, Philip and Daniel Seguin.

CONTRIBUTOR — **Virginia Lewise Horger Grogan** ("Ginny Lew") was born in Virginia. Her father, Lewis Horger, was born in Texas, and her mother, Virginia Dorlon, was born in Troy, N.Y. — the great-great-granddaughter of William and Ann Cluett. After studying mathematics, she worked for G.E. in Philadelphia for 2 years, but then turned her attention to working with youth — native Americans in South Dakota, troubled children in Seattle, WN, and Latinos in Denver, CO.

Her interest in family history began with a visit from her cousin, Emily Dorlon Rodemann, in the early 1980's. They did research, contacted relatives, and published a family newsletter, which included information about the Dorlons, Cadbys, and Cluetts. After transcribing (and then photocopying and distributing) original letters sent to and from Emily Cluett Cadby and her Cluett family in Troy, Ginny "met" her 3rd cousin, Robert Cluett IV and his daughter, Marjorie.

Ginny has three children: Lewis (deceased), Kathleen Andriunas (Colorado) and Jeffrey (Oregon). She now lives in Highlands Ranch, Colorado.

www.ingramcontent.com/pod-product-compliance
Lightning Source LLC
Chambersburg PA
CBHW060458010526
44118CB00018B/2462

* 9 7 8 0 9 9 4 0 1 0 6 9 8 *